from the
INSIDE
Out

✝ faith books & MORE

Suwanee, Georgia

Michelle Alden

First published by Faith Books & MORE
ISBN 978-0-98457793-4

Printed in the United States of America.

This book is printed on acid-free paper.

3255 Lawrenceville-Suwanee Rd.
Suite P250
Suwanee, GA 30024
publishing@faithbooksandmore.com
www.faithbooksandmore.com

DEDICATION

For my brothers Jack and Mike, we lived a lifetime together
before adoption seperated us. I love you guys, and I just
want to remind you that God knows every story from the
inside out.

Love,
Michelle

ACKNOWLEDGEMENTS

I want to thank my friends who prayed for and supported me throughout this process and encouraged me to keep going and keep writing: Jenn Austring, Sherri Coffield, Julie Carr, and my Camp Esther sisters. I will be forever grateful to Royal Family Kids Camp and the coureagous kids, victims of abuse that touch my life year after year. Thanks to Talitha Roustin who provided hilarious stories from her son to add humor to this story, and for Carol Gloetzner and Megan Walsh who answered questions about adopting their children and gave additional insight from experience about what the kids needed the most. Also huge thanks to Sherri Brooks, who spent hours chatting with me about her two adopted girls, and for sharing her stories and some of the daily struggles. I so appreciate how much hope she gives her girls and other parents who want to adopt. Thanks to my adoptive parents Bill and Paula Jones for giving me a home, a family and a new life. To my husband, Tim who listened to the story all through the process and encouraged me to follow my dream to write this book. Lastly I have thank my daughters: Bekah, Jenah, Naomi and Anne for believing in me as a mom and a writer, for spending endless hours talking about this family in the book as if we actually knew them and for pushing me to make it possible for other people to read.

chapter

Rachel stood in the doorway of the family room and surveyed the scene. TJ, her husband of almost five years, watched the television with great concentration even though the game hadn't started yet. Rachel knew he liked the pre-game show almost as much as the game itself. It was mid-November, and true to family tradition, the Keytons were gearing up for Monday night football.

Occasionally TJ interjected a comment about something the kids said. Mary, his youngest daughter and the youngest of their combined six children, cuddled up next to him, her curly blond hair resting on his shoulder. She focused on a book, as was characteristic for her. How good the game was versus how good the book was determined whether she continued to read after the kickoff. Only Beth and Hope, their college girls, wouldn't be home tonight.

Beth, Rachel's daughter, a senior at Ole' Miss, was finishing up her student teaching. She had left for school in the years before TJ and his kids had passed the whole football craze to Rachel and her girls.

Hope, TJ's oldest daughter, just starting her first year at Belmont University in Nashville, would be calling to check in later. She had been home over the weekend, but as usual, had to head back to school for Monday classes. She wouldn't get to watch football with the family for a while. But she had a group of kids she hung with on Monday nights and would certainly be watching the Tennessee Titans with them tonight.

The Titans were the team the whole family rooted for. TJ's girls had grown up watching football with their dad and no matter how busy their lives became, they always stopped and joined together to continue the tradition. Rachel loved it.

When Rachel had first met TJ, she knew him as Troy Keyton, country music star. As one of the most well-known, highly paid country music artists for over fifteen years, his was a household name. His credits included more than twenty top single hits, numerous career titles such as Entertainer of the Year, Country Music Hall of Fame Artist, and Male Vocalist of the Year. She had listened to his music and been to his concerts before but meeting him had not even been on her radar of hopes.

Now, four years later, here she was, spending her days and nights with the man of her dreams. Within a year of meeting, they had married and TJ had totally quit the music business the following year. He spent his days coaching their kids' softball teams, mentoring young men and managing Hope Enterprises, Inc., a non-profit organization Rachel had started to help families and kids.

Hope Enterprises was involved in programs and camps locally in Nashville, throughout Tennessee and Colorado where Rachel was from and just about every state in between. Although Rachel still had her hands in it, Hope E. was mostly run by TJ with his endless supply of resources. As she watched him now Rachel felt, as she always had, that Troy Keyton was at his absolute best in the role of dad and family man.

Waiting for the snacks she was baking, Rachel lingered near the doorway, her eyes resting affectionately on Naomi and Gracie. Both had boys over, Tucker and Danny, whom she knew well from football and baseball teams TJ had coached at the high school. Danny had been mentored through the fatherless generation project TJ had started. Since Danny and Tucker graduated in June, they helped out at Hope Enterprises with mentoring and coaching younger boys. They shared an apartment near the community college they attended, getting their core classes out of the way.

Tucker and Naomi had been going out since before

graduation, through summer and fall. Naomi, Rachel's middle daughter, lived at home and worked fulltime at the local animal shelter. She was gifted with animals and children. Rachel counted on her to help in her equine-assisted therapy programs.

Rachel sighed as she watched Tucker put his arm around Naomi. It was bitter-sweet, the kids growing up. She was thankful Tucker was such a nice kid. Still, she hoped they would give themselves more time before getting too serious about their relationship. Naomi was undecided about college and her future and Tucker was thinking about pursuing a teaching degree so he could coach high school sports.

Gracie and Danny stated more than once that they were just friends, but from where Rachel stood, she could see they liked each other a great deal. She knew for a fact Gracie was interested in more than friendship. A couple of times she had wondered to Rachel why he hadn't asked her out. All through high school Danny hung close to TJ. Like Tucker, Danny hoped to become a coach. Rachel knew Danny's family situation was unstable. TJ was a father figure to him and their home was a second family, perhaps more real than his own. Rachel thought Danny's hesitance to date Gracie had more to do with his fear of damaging his ties with TJ than anything else.

Gracie was still in high school, a senior. She had been especially close to her mother, Kris, who had died in an automobile accident three years before Rachel had met TJ. With her blond hair and fair complexion, Gracie favored Kris. Blending their families had cost Rachel and TJ a lot of care, prayer and tender understanding, especially for Gracie and Rachel. But they had finally found a comfortable relationship, one where Gracie let down her guard enough to admit her frustration about Danny. Watching them talk and joke around, Rachel thought it was just a matter of time before he expressed to Gracie how he felt about her.

Emily, Rachel's youngest, was also a senior. She squinted at her iPod, ignoring her sisters and the boys. All of Rachel's girls looked like her, but Beth and Emily shared the most similar features. Small-boned and energetic, Emily's light brown hair and blue eyes sparkled. Numerous boys called her each night, but Emily kept them at bay. Rarely did she invite just one to do anything. When she had friends over, it was usually a gang of them and almost always geared around an event.

She had a band that included several guys. They often got together to practice downstairs in the studio TJ had set up. Of their six kids, Emily was the only one interested in a musical career. TJ told Rachel when they first got to know each other that he never wanted any of his kids to follow him into the music business. Now with Emily so eager and talented, TJ found himself in a tough spot. He had the contacts to help her get started, but he opposed the idea. It was a sore spot between them at times.

Meanwhile, Emily used her talents on the worship team at church, leading music at camps, writing songs and singing at school events and talent shows. It wasn't going to satisfy her forever, and Rachel knew when the time came TJ would be the one to help her through the maze of the music industry. How and when was something they would have to hash out.

Emily scooted over by Mary and tried to pull her out of her book to show her something on the iPod. Mary looked at it and they both laughed. Technically, they were all watching the game or would be as soon as it started. Rachel remained near the kitchen, waiting for popcorn to finish up in the microwave. It was her duty to bring food to starving football fans. She tucked her light brown hair behind her ears as she bent to check the goodies in the oven.

Officially, TJ was retired from the music business, although around their home he was always singing something. When they were dating TJ would sing to Rachel over the phone. He still sang to her sometimes while she was falling asleep, and in his most romantic moments, he wrote songs for her. He never went more than a few days without playing his guitar and had taught Rachel to play a bit. She had little time or talent but enjoyed singing with him in the car or when they had the chance to sit and strum.

Lately TJ and Emily had been "jamming" together. Throughout the summer their respective music buddies often held these events around bonfires on their property. Country music ran deep in all their hearts and retired or not, music remained part of their lives.

Rachel, a therapist who worked with families, had met TJ because of her work with abused women and children. Good friends of TJ's and his first wife's, singer Katrina Metcalf and her husband Mike, had heard Rachel on a national radio program. They invited her and her girls to visit them in Tennessee.

During that visit, the Metcafes introduced Rachel to Troy Keyton and to his nickname of TJ, which Mike had bestowed on him years ago. They claimed the introduction was purely business, but Rachel had her doubts. She thought Tina might have been playing match-maker all along and she still gave her friend a hard time about it, even though she would be forever in her debt. Who would have guessed they would later live less than ten miles from the Metcafes and that their kids would attend the same schools? Hope and the Metcafe's daughter, Laney, became best friends and attended Ole' Miss together. Less than a year from that first meeting, Rachel married TJ and she and her daughters moved to Tennessee. Rachel loved their 900-acre farm, their house, their blended family and the life they continued to build together. She knew it was crazy, but then so were the chances of an average girl from a small town who ran a non-profit organization meeting and falling in love with an American idol. She and TJ would hate it if any of their daughters did the same thing. But it worked for them. Rachel was sure their success was due to their mutual faith and strong commitment to family.

TJ hadn't planned on quitting his music career but when he did, the benefits to the family were huge. Their combined efforts in helping kids opened numerous doors for them. They both ran camps and trained volunteers all over the country. They worked hard for their own family and for others. Their kids participated in the camps and helped on different levels. TJ and Rachel had both come from tough childhoods so they were fully engaged in creating the kind of family they wanted. As she took fresh baked cookies from the oven and surveyed all the snacks on the counter, Rachel thought their life was pretty good. Whenever anyone asked TJ how it worked for them, he replied, "Well, it helps a lot that my wife is a therapist and so damn good at what she does."

That answer was almost laughable to Rachel, who knew that wasn't even close to the truth. She always said, "It is love and faith—from the inside out."

Returning to the family room with a big tray of snacks, Rachel watched her husband teasing and clowning around with the kids. She was continually captivated by his natural good looks. He'd turned fifty in September and joked about getting old. But he kept himself in good shape, jogging and working on the farm. His dark brown hair was thinning and his sideburns were mostly gray, but to Rachel, he seemed to get more handsome each year. Her eyes lingered on his face. She loved his deep brown eyes and easy going smile that brought out a dimple like the ones his daughters shared. His rugged masculinity still held the power to make her heart leap. He had traded his fame for family, but his presence was still larger than life. In Rachel's eyes, he just kept getting better.

TJ glanced her way, winked and motioned for her to join him. "Come on, Babe. It's the Titans tonight. You don't want to miss kick off!"

He scooted closer to Mary to make room for Rachel on his other side. He playfully patted the space between himself and the arm of the couch. "I saved you a seat." His brown eyes danced.

"Food is ready," she said to the kids.

Cuddling beside TJ, she said, "I was just enjoying the view." He pulled her close and kissed her. The girls yelled, pretending to be grossed out. Mary hid her face behind his back. But TJ just kissed her again.

"Kick off!" Naomi yelled to distract them.

Rachel grinned at her husband. "What did we ever do on Monday nights before we met you, Mr. Keyton?"

"I have no idea," he said. "What do people do on Monday night if they don't watch football?" The question was directed toward everyone in the room.

The boys beamed at him. "What does that even mean?" Danny said lightheartedly, shaking his head in disbelief that such creatures could exist. "You love it, too, don't you, Mrs. Keyton?"

"Oh, yeah," Rachel quickly replied. "I love everything about Monday nights at this house."

TJ pulled her close again, cheering as the Titans received the kickoff to start the game.

chapter

Rachel was up early. She pulled on her favorite old jeans, sweatshirt and baseball cap, grabbed her journal and slipped on her boots. She headed toward the barn, one of her preferred places on the property to pray, think and write. Even though the weather was growing colder, she still went there. It was one place she could be alone and not distracted. TJ had asked her to consider something and unless she took the time to write and pray it through, she would never have a solid answer for him. This decision would affect all their lives and she needed God's wisdom, guidance and assurance.

About a year before, TJ had approached her about adopting two little boys they had met through the Fatherless Generation Program in Nashville, part of the inner city day camp he sponsored. The brothers had experienced really tough lives for children so young. Their history included abuse, neglect and ultimately abandonment. Their father was in prison and their mother had given up her rights to raise them. Rachel knew them from participation in various programs and TJ saw them several times a week. They had met with a caseworker and were planning a day visit in the spring.

TJ and Rachel had been discussing adoption all year, taking classes and going through preliminary requirements. Rachel wanted to do it, but she was aware how difficult it would be. Until she could really lay it all out before her Father and have His final word she couldn't go any further. She knew how intense and challenging this would be for the family. To rest her fears and doubts she needed to know deep inside that the next step was guided by God. If God was in it she knew no matter what they faced it would be all right.

As she wrote out the things she knew about the boys—how cute they were and how much TJ wanted to do this—she smiled. She remembered Ricky's laughter when he got to ride the pony on his first trip to the farm with some other boys. She pondered the expression in Ben's eyes, the depth there of one so young who had seen too much. Something about Ben made Rachel want to hold him close, tell him it would be okay and that he could let go because they would fight the world for him. "He thinks he has to be so strong," she wrote in her journal. She also wrote that he reminded her of TJ. Although there was no blood relation, no one would ever doubt TJ and Ben were father and son. She knew her own heart and she knew the boys. Adopting them had already found a hold inside her.

The stillness of the morning and the smell of hay and horses filled her senses. The peaceful assurance taking over her heart brought Rachel to a quiet resolve. She would do as she felt her Father was asking. She would be a mama to those little boys. In doing so, she and TJ would face unpleasant memories from their pasts that would challenge them. Their family would not only grow but would change.

Though aware of the gravity of the decision, Rachel couldn't help feeling excited. She had experienced childbirth and step-motherhood. She was open to experiencing the adoptive aspect of parenting, too. Ben and Ricky were darling. They had managed to climb into her heart the moment she saw them. And then there was TJ. She couldn't think of a better man to be their daddy. His excitement and assurance from the first time he mentioned it to her had never waned. He loved his family and he was so good with kids. None of her doubts were about TJ or his role in all of this.

She leaned back against a hay bale and breathed deeply. "Okay, God. I know this is what you want. I'm game. I just didn't want my own desires to get in the way. I know you are leading us to this place. When it gets hard or we have our doubts, I will go back to this moment when I felt your peace and knew for sure you called us into their lives and them into ours." She opened her hands and lifted them toward God. "Whatever it takes, Lord, pour out your love on us so we can bring healing to these two boys." Rachel wrote what she had said out loud and noted the resolve she felt. She finished by writing about the boys and what she hoped for them.

The boys' caseworker, Lori, was a friend of Rachel's. She began working hard to get TJ and Rachel through the required process for foster parenting. The boys had just been switched to yet another home. Rachel and TJ didn't want to move them again until they were sure this was where they would stay. Meanwhile, they had several visits with the boys and were planning a couple of outings this winter before the home visit in the spring.

They could take the boys as foster parents without a long-term commitment. But that had never been okay with her or TJ. They felt strongly that it was in the best interest of the boys, and for their family, to take them only if it was for the long haul. Rachel believed anything less than a forever home would only bring more pain and turmoil. They were taking things slowly so everyone felt they had choices. The boys, she, TJ and their kids should all be in agreement. Even so, for Rachel is was an all or nothing deal. No thoughts of, "We'll see if it works."

That very idea baffled Rachel. What did it mean anyway, if the boys were good enough they would keep them? Otherwise, they would toss them back?

"Can you imagine if all kids were in families based on that kind of agreement?" TJ once asked. At a family meeting with Rachel and the girls, he stated firmly, "If we do this, it's for better or worse, whatever it takes, or we don't do it at all."

Rachel agreed. Finishing up her writing, she closed the journal and stood, stretching her back. She crossed to the window of the loft and looked out. The sun was rising higher in the clear sky, but frost still laced the grass. She loved all the seasons on the farm. She scanned the arena where she worked with kids and families.

The horses stomped around, waiting impatiently for their morning meal. TJ had ten quarter horses and she had her four that were her therapy partners. She heard TJ whistle for the dogs as he came out of the house and strode toward the barn. Rachel thought about TJ's two hounds that had died last year a few months apart. He loved bird hunting and his hounds had been close companions. He had tried to teach Rachel's black lab, Maverick, but he wasn't very good.

Maverick jumped excitedly around TJ's feet. TJ had given up on training the lab and tried working with Lady, his six-month-old blue tick hound. In her he had discovered a new hunting buddy. She fell over Maverick, vying for TJ's attention. Deeply satisfied with the answers in her heart and wanting to inform TJ of her thoughts, she turned from the window and headed down to greet him. As soon as he saw her face, Rachel could tell he knew. He grinned at her. She nodded and he scooped her into a strong embrace. Rachel laughed then playfully begged him to let her go. She could scarcely breathe he was holding her so tightly.

"I knew it!" he told her. "I know this is totally the right thing for us to do. At least you didn't take as long as you did when I asked you to marry me," he teased.

"Yeah, well, this was easier." She kissed his cheek. "So, I guess we just have to set up those day visits and finish up our classes and home inspections."

"Lori thinks they can get us approved by the end of next month. Then the boys could come out in the spring as we planned." TJ gazed at Rachel. She took his hand and returned his intensity. All sign of joking was gone. "Wow. Now it is kind of hitting me."

"Oh, Hon," she said tenderly, "it may seem fast, but jumping in all the way with you like this is like watching something I've dreamed of coming true. I really did always want to adopt but I seriously doubted I would ever be in a place where I could do it."

"Doesn't it seem we should have some kind of ceremony of vows to each other right now? I mean, we are starting this journey and we have no idea where it will take us or how it might affect us. It just seems like we should be doing more than signing papers."

"I know what you mean."

"We could create our own, you know," he said. "I heard about one family that celebrates 'Gotcha Day' every year on the day they adopted their kids. We could do something like that."

"I would have liked that when I was a kid." Rachel mused. He searched her face. "What are you thinking?"

TJ sighed contentedly and wrapped his arms around her waist. "I am thinking that you are the most amazing woman I have ever known. And that I am really glad you married me. There is no one I would rather be with on this adventure." He kissed her with resolve.

She pulled away before his enthusiasm made her lose track of her senses. "I wanted to tell you that, too. You know, Baby, this adventure may stretch us to the limits on all sides, but I feel—from the inside out—there is nothing else I would rather do than walk this path with you."

He took her hand and together they started toward the house. "Let's tell the girls as soon as we can. Then let's decide together some ways we can help those boys feel they are really home. I think the girls will want to be part of it all. They might even have ideas how we can seal this commitment. What do you think?"

Rachel nodded and smiled up at him. Her heart was full. Life was full.

chapter

The Little Girl

She stood just inside the big door. One small suitcase held everything she owned. Nothing more, nothing less. Her name was Rachel. She was painfully aware of her thin body and uncombed stringy blonde hair with bangs cut short by her own hand. She felt small and ugly standing on the threshold of a new home and a new life.

Her eyes stung as tears threatened. She wasn't sad. She was terrified. This was her chance to start over. But even at six she knew there was a greater possibility she would mess it up than that it would actually work out to be her forever home. She had learned a long time ago never to wish for anything too much.

"Let me help you put your things away," the stranger who was going to be her new mother said.

Rachel held tightly to her suitcase. She had immediate reservations about this lady's intentions. She was sure that despite the smile and offer to help, her new mom, like all the others, probably wouldn't like her. Maybe the woman didn't really want her to be there. Reading people's moods and looking for acceptance were second nature.

"I can do it myself." Rachel pulled away. She was, after all, almost seven. She needed to establish her independence right away. Plus, taking care of herself was one of the few skills she was sure about.

Rachel felt the lady tense. She discerned a familiar gut reaction. Already the lady didn't like her. Worried but without options, she followed the mom to her new room.

She had visited here once before. She knew the Lewis's had horses and a pool. She would get her own room. She had never had her own anything. She hoped it was a good place and she wanted to live here though she had no idea what it all meant. She had no experiences of love and acceptance to allow her anything other than a certain dread that once they got to know her they, too, would send her away.

Looking back years later, Rachel remembered nothing else about that day when she went to live with her adoptive family. Sometimes she wasn't even sure about those fleeting memories. What she never forgot, though, was how totally lost she felt, how frightened and small, especially under the scrutiny of her new mother's gaze. All the other details of that moment were gone. She knew her adoptive father must have been there, as well as her brother, John. But she couldn't place them in the picture at all.

At six years old, Rachel had stepped into a new life. She was just a little girl who more than anything needed to know she was wanted, valued and loved. But what Rachel remembered most was the absence of hugs, acceptance, and love. Since she had only her previous experiences to guide her, Rachel did what she could to keep herself safe. And on that first day at her new home she made up her mind to stand strong and never let them know she cared if they kept her or not.

chapter

The two of them stood close together which made them look even more small and unsure. They were excited, Rachel could see it in their eyes, but she also saw mistrust and uncertainty. She smiled encouragingly at them and hoped for the best. Their eagerness to see inside such a huge house was taking over their fear. They gazed wide-eyed at the soaring ceilings, elegant hardwood floors and huge staircase that could be seen from the entryway.

Ben was six years old and Ricky had just turned five. Rachel knew they were trying to wait patiently as she and TJ talked with their caseworker, Lori. She was dropping them off for a day visit and would be back before supper. The boys had been told the Keytons wanted to adopt them and this was their first time seeing what could be their new home. So far, everything seemed to be a go.

Rachel could feel their childish energy threatening to burst as they took in their surroundings. As Lori talked with TJ, she took a moment to study the boys. Ben stood slightly taller than Ricky with a stockier build. His muted brown hair hung above dark, sober eyes. Both boys had round faces, like TJ's. With skin tone lighter than Ben's, Ricky's eager smile displayed dimples. His blue eyes seemed less reserved, too. The boys really didn't look like brothers except for the shape of their faces.

Rachel tried to catch Ben's eye and smile at him again but he looking around as if trying to decide what might be around the corner in what must have seemed a massive palace. Of course, they had probably never seen a house this big. She hoped their sense of adventure would win out over their fears.

Ricky hopped on one foot then the other. Ben nudged him to keep still and Rachel heard him whisper, "Hold your horses, Ricky!"

Mary came bounding down the stairs, eager to meet the

boys and begged to take them on a tour right away. Finishing up chatting with Lori, TJ turned his attention on the boys and asked if he could tag along on Mary's tour. The boys were delighted.

"Come on, men." TJ and the boys followed Mary. "Let's go."

Rachel laughed. She never got tired of watching TJ with kids.

The boys had been on the horse part of the property before, but they had never been in the house. Rachel had the kids from the city program up a couple of times a month during the summer to work with the horses. Some of the kids did equine therapy. Often their families participated as well. As city kids, many of them had never been out to the country and certainly none of them had seen a place quite like the Keytons'. The lush green horse pastures ran along both sides of the paved driveway which was nearly a mile long. White fencing outlined the grassy spaces. The huge modern barn and covered arena held kids spellbound when they first saw them. Rachel used to tease TJ that it was the horse facilities that won her over and was the real reason she had left Colorado to marry him.

Rachel looked around the kitchen and saw its extravagance afresh through their young eyes. She was glad they had waited to bring the boys here. She thought it better they decided to come live with them before being overwhelmed with the huge house and all the material benefits they would receive as part of the Keytons. From the outside the house looked like an old southern plantation mansion, three stories high, white colonial pillars in front and wide wrap-around porches. Inside it was just as spacious. For those two little foster boys who had never had a real home of their own, let alone their own beds, it probably seemed like a palace.

Rachel could hear voices coming up from the recreation

room, gym and studio in the basement. She put cookies she had made with Naomi the night before on a plate at the center of the table. She added fruit, juice and milk. She had seen the boys eat before. Though they were small, they never seemed to get full.

Rachel's cell rang. Hope was on her way. Gracie and Emily were working with friends on senior projects and would be home around noon. Naomi would be able to see the boys in the afternoon when her shift was over.

Rachel added a few more cookies to the plate. TJ would want to take the boys to the pond to go fishing. Rachel and the girls would follow on the horses for a picnic in the "back forty."

It was the end of March and the weather was holding out for them, a warm spring day, especially for Tennessee where it tended to be rainy this time of year. If it had rained, Rachel was sure TJ would have gone fishing anyway. Fishing with his sons was something he had always dreamed about. He took all the girls fishing and camping with him, and on occasion they even hunted with him. Deep inside though, she knew he was completely taken with the idea of doing those things with his sons.

Rachel also knew from experience with her clients that had adopted kids that idyllic family moments with troubled kids were few and far between. Nevertheless, she hoped they'd be making memories together soon.

That father part of TJ was so attractive to Rachel she couldn't put it into words. It stirred her deeply. From the start, they'd shared a love for parenting and a desire to build a family. They had found family to be the most therapeutic component of their lives. Rachel had to admit the possibility of raising these boys with TJ was something she greatly desired.

As she came around the corner of the stairs she could hear them in the band room. She quietly opened the door and

peered in. Mary helped Ricky get situated with the drums
while TJ showed Ben how to place his fingers on the guitar.
Ricky reached for the sticks. Mary patiently explained to him
about each of the drums and how to hit them and the cymbals
correctly. Rachel studied the boys with swelling heart. They
were such cute little guys.

Ben listened to TJ with a serious face. His fingers couldn't
quite reach around the neck of the guitar and manage to press
the strings so TJ held the chords while Ben strummed. Ricky
started hitting the drums with great enthusiasm. He wasn't at
all serious. He laughed boisterously as he crashed the
drumstick on the cymbals, thrilled at the powerful sounds he
was able to make. Ben looked over, obviously annoyed. "Knock
it off, Ricky!" But Ricky proceeded to whack the drums a few
more good licks.

"Time for a snack," Rachel called. This interrupted Ben's
rebukes and gave Mary a chance to take control of the sticks.
"Time to eat!" TJ added with enthusiasm, most likely to
distract Ben from his frustration with Ricky. TJ put the guitar
back on its stand and herded the boys toward the door.

chapter

Sunday night the girls found their places around the family table. TJ smiled at Rachel and took her hand. She caressed the back of his lightly with her thumb. Finally they were all seated, even Hope, who had delayed going back to school so she could be there for the family meeting. As soon as they were ready, TJ called Beth on the speaker phone so she could be part of the conversation, too.

When TJ and Rachel got married, he was already having family meetings each week with his girls and he was adamant that they continue. There were times no one seemed to want to be there and there were of course some meetings that ended badly with one or more persons upset, bored or frustrated. Other meetings were light and carefree. But all were vital to family discussions and planning.

They had been looking forward to this particular assembly as they would finalize plans for bringing Ben and Ricky into the family. It wasn't their first meeting about the boys. TJ and Rachel felt they all needed to be in agreement about this adoption from the beginning. It was an important meeting as they moved forward.

They all waited, listening to the phone ring through the speaker. When Beth picked up, she sounded out of breath.

"Hi, Dad," she answered. "I left my cell phone in Laney's backpack. Sorry."

"Hello, Beth."

It amazed Rachel how quickly her girls had accepted TJ as their dad. Maybe since they hadn't known a father before it was easier. Their dad had left when Emily was five and even before that he had hardly been around. Rachel feared he would resurface at some point, but he never did. It had been more difficult for TJ's girls to get close to Rachel.

"Hey, girl," Rachel said.

"We are all here." TJ motioned toward the others at the table to say hello. Everyone chimed in, all talking at once. "Say hi to your mama and sisters."

"Hi, y'all," Beth replied. "Okay. I don't have a lot of time. What's up?"

TJ started. Beth knew about the boys and had met them briefly over Christmas break. He told her they had visited the farm. The other girls piped in with stories about the picnic and how cute the boys were. Beth asked questions about their ages and personalities since her field of study was teaching with an emphasis on child development in hopes of becoming a school counselor.

"So, we are here to discuss finalizing the adoption." TJ brought them to the topic at hand. "Your mother and I, we want everyone to be a part of it."

"I am curious about your thoughts," Rachel said, talking to all the kids. "I am wondering what you thought when you met them and how the day went."

Emily, as usual, jumped in first. "I thought they were so cute!"

"Yeah," Naomi agreed. "Did you notice how Ricky kept watching Ben and trying to do everything he did?"

"What I noticed was how Ben watched Dad and tried to copy him," Gracie chimed in. "They are so small. Really, Daddy, I think it would be totally cool to adopt them."

TJ grinned over at Rachel. "What do you think, Mama?" Knowing she would have the most concerns, he squeezed her hand to encourage her to speak her mind.

"Well, I can't deny that my heart is taken by those boys. I am so glad we are going to have them here. But I have to say to all of you that this decision will affect all of our lives. Even though Beth is not at home and you girls will be leaving in the next few years, you will all be impacted in one way or another if these boys become your brothers. I am not saying I don't want it or that it will be bad. I just know they will require something from all of us. And ideally I want all of us to embrace that challenge, even those that aren't living here for most of it. Does that make sense? If we do this, we all do it. They aren't just our sons or TJ's boys or one of my projects. They need a family—a mama, a daddy and sisters. And that means for better or for worse. And to be honest, with their backgrounds, it could be a lot of worse."

"You want to do it, right, Mom?" Beth asked. "I mean, we already decided that, right?"

"Yeah, I do, hon. And yes, having the boys over and asking them about it really meant we were going forward with it. I just want you to know it affects us all. It can't just be because they are cute or that your dad and I want to do it. And when we are tired or hurt by something they do or say, and when we wonder why in the world we willingly chose this path, we need to be able to come back to this moment—this assurance that we agreed together and felt led by God and had His promise to help us see it through. The confidence has to come from the inside out."

The faces around the table were contemplative. TJ put his arm around Rachel's shoulders. "Let's all pray together about this," he said, "and be willing to stand together." One by one, they stood and joined hands.

"I'm standing too, Dad," Beth said. And TJ prayed for his family.

chapter

The Little Boy

The little boy hid in the closet of the room he shared with his younger sister, Julie. He held her close to his trembling body, trying the best he could to keep her from hearing the fight in the other room. He pressed one of her ears against his chest and covered the other with his hand, tucking his head close to hers to smother the sound of the ugly words his stepfather hurled at their mother. He wanted to cry but he had to be strong for Julie, maybe for his mama, and certainly for himself.

Troy wished he could take his frightened sister and run far, far away from all the fighting, especially the yelling and hitting. He hated his own fear and the tears that threatened to escape as he tried to protect his sister, all the while worrying about his mother. He could hear her soothing yet strained voice as she tried to calm George. She pleaded with him to sit down and watch TV while she cleaned up. It wouldn't work. Troy was only six and he knew it wouldn't work. When George was mad and came home smelling like the bottles he drank from every night it never worked to beg and plead. Troy hated that the only thing he could do was hide like a baby. He wouldn't cry though. He told himself over and over, "Big boys don't cry."

There was a loud crash and more bad words. Julie pulled away to look around. She was only four. It was Troy's job to look out for her. He tried to pull her back in close. But he wondered if he should go check on his mama. What should he do? Should he stay hidden and protect Julie or should he help his mother? His body trembled again as George called his mama another bad word. Then he heard the thing he most dreaded, the unmistakable sound of George's huge fist striking the soft flesh and bones of their mama's beautiful face.

Troy let go of his sister and whispered for her to stay put.

He ran out to the kitchen. His mother lay on the floor in a crumpled heap. George moved toward her to hurt her again. Forgetting his fear, Troy rushed toward him.

"Leave her alone!" Troy barreled into his stepfather with all the force in his little body. It caught the big man off guard momentarily then he regained his balance.

"Look at you, you little sh–!" He laughed, his voice slurred. Though he staggered, Troy knew his ability to cause pain and suffering was right on the mark. He held the boy off easily with one hand. "You want a piece of this?" George laughed again at Troy's efforts to protect his mother. Then George's strong right hand slammed across the side of his face. That was all it took, one blow, and Troy went down to the floor near his mother. She struggled up to help her son, scooting her body toward him. George kicked her in the back. She sank back down with moan and lost consciousness.

Troy lay on the floor between his mother's limp arms. His head hurt and he couldn't stop the tears flowing down his face from pain, anger and hurt so deep inside no one could touch it. George turned toward the bedroom doorway. Troy squeezed his eyes shut tight when he noticed Julie standing there.

chapter

Getting all the paperwork completed and the home study done seemed to take forever. The girls jumped in with decorating and shopping for their new brothers. But once the family was ready, it was still a waiting game. Social Services didn't want to move the boys until school was out so they were in no hurry. The family had weekly contact with them, but Rachel had accepted the fact that the move would not happen until June.

Then suddenly, everything happened at once. The home the boys had been in was closing unexpectedly and all the children had to be placed in new locations. With only a few weeks of school left, social services wanted to keep the boys close by until they were out for the summer. Since they attended a school in Nashville they would have to move to a temporary home.

Rachel advocated strongly that boys not have to make more than one move. "Lori, you know those boys don't need to be bumped around like that," Rachel insisted. "They should only have to move once, and it should be directly into our home!" TJ agreed and added his own arguments.

Finally social services relented. The only stipulation was that the Keytons drive Ben into Nashville to school each day so he could complete kindergarten. Since Ricky's pre-school daycare was not mandatory, they had the option to keep him enrolled or wait to start school in the fall. Rachel would rather keep both boys home to get settled and then start fresh with a new school nearby, but since the boys were wards of the state, they had to comply.

It was May twelfth, a Tuesday night, when Ben and Ricky arrived with all their belongings in a medium sized suitcase and a black plastic garbage bag. TJ had gotten the call at 4:00 that afternoon that the boys would be there in an hour or so.

After all the waiting they had only an hour's notice.

Thankfully, the Keytons were ready. They had been anticipating getting the boys as soon as possible. Rachel knew foster children generally moved from home to home with very few personal belongings so she wasn't sure what they would arrive with. She and TJ had bought clothing and toiletries for each boy.

Ben's and Ricky's rooms were on the main floor near Rachel's and TJ's master suite. Finding out what most interested the boys, Hope and Naomi had come up with ideas for each of their rooms. Gracie, Mary and Emily had joined the fun of creating and decorating. Ben was a huge sports fan so the girls found things from teams he told them he liked. They chose a green bedspread that looked like a football grid. They selected a Nerf basketball and hoop as well. TJ added a real football and helmet as well as a baseball and glove. Rachel teased TJ that he was having way too much fun for someone that claimed to hate shopping.

That evening when the family showed Ben his room, his eyes lit up. But he stood frozen in the doorway, scanning the football, baseball and basketball posters. He seemed almost afraid everything would vanish if he touched anything.

He turned to his little brother. "Do you like it Ricky?"

Ricky nodded.

Rachel realized the boys assumed they would both be staying in the room. She knew placing them in separate rooms might be difficult at first, but she felt strongly that they needed their own space and identity.

"Guess what, Ricky?" She touched his shoulder gently.

"You have a room made just for you, too. Do you want to see it?"

He looked up at her and nodded.

"Ben, do you want to see Ricky's room? It is right next to yours." Ben put his arm around his brother.

"It's okay if he stays with me," he said protectively.

Rachel lowered to one knee to be at the boys' level. "That is so great that you want to share with your brother." She placed her hand cautiously on Ben's back. "I'm sure you will have lots of sleepovers in each others' rooms. The girls do that, too. But Ricky has a room with some of his favorite things. Come see." She stood up and offered him her hand.

He ignored it and folded his arms across his small chest. But he moved to go with them to see the other room. Rachel gave him his space knowing how his background had shaped his responses. She understood the importance of his independence and his role as the older brother.

The whole group hung back a little to watch Ricky's face as he looked into his room. Ricky wanted more than anything to be a cowboy and had been thrilled that he was going to live at a place with horses. He had told Mary on his first visit that he wanted his own horse. His room had been designed for an aspiring cowboy with pictures on the walls of real cowboys roping, steer wrestling and bull-riding. Several model horses stood regally atop the dresser and a border of running horses circled the top of the walls. The bed looked like blue jeans. TJ had bought Ricky a pair of boots and a cowboy hat that looked like a replica of the one he used to wear in his concerts. Rachel smiled as Ricky's face lit up.

"Oh, wow!" he kept saying, then over and over as if convincing himself, "Mine, mine, mine." TJ put his arm around Rachel's shoulders. The girls beamed.

Ben stood silently. Rachel watched him taking in each thing in Ricky's room. Then he turned and went back to his own. Rachel caught TJ's eye and he nodded to her that he would follow Ben. Rachel had looked at Ben's file and talked to Lori numerous times about the abuse he had suffered from his birth mother. When Rachel had been around the boys, Ben had always been polite and friendly. But seeing her as his next foster mother, Rachel saw all the signs of mistrust in his guarded behavior. Having been adopted at almost the same age, she knew deep in her heart that his biggest need was simply time to trust, especially since he had been so hurt and felt so rejected by his mother.

As TJ brushed past her to follow Ben to his room, Rachel squeezed his arm in a silent bond. The girls were so busy watching Ricky explore they didn't notice that Ben and TJ had left. Mary took down the model horses and she and Ricky galloped them around the room while the others watched and laughed. Glancing down the hall, Rachel saw TJ leaning in Ben's doorway talking quietly.

After watching the girls' play with Ricky, Rachel asked if he and Ben had eaten supper. He looked up from his horses and nodded his head vigorously. "Yes! Hungry!"

She laughed and said she would get some food ready and call them when it was time to eat. Naomi and Mary went back to engaging Ricky in play and conversation while Gracie and Emily said they would help prepare dinner.

Rachel paused at Ben's room and looked in. Ben sat on his bed holding his new football. He had his helmet on. TJ sat on the floor nearby. They were talking about something, probably football. They both looked up when she said she was going to make something to eat.

"Good idea, Mama," TJ said. "Are you hungry, little man?"

Ben looked at Rachel with the most serious eyes she had ever seen. He slowly nodded.

TJ answered for both of them. "Yep, we're hungry!"

Rachel grinned and just shook her head. Ben might be unsure, but TJ was beside himself with joy.

"Thought so. I'm thinking hamburgers and French fries. What do you think, Ben?" She knew they were his favorites.

"Can mine be a cheeseburger?" he asked somberly.

"Cheese is definitely an option," she told him.

"Okay." He nodded and almost smiled.

"Thanks, Babe," TJ said and Rachel left to get the food ready.

The boys ate heartily. If they were worried about staying at a new place it wasn't affecting their appetites. The girls questioned them more about their favorite things.

As Rachel ate, she basked in the thrill of seeing the kids interact. She loved listening and watching the boys becoming more comfortable.

They were eating later than usual and by the time they finished it was nearly 7:30. TJ instructed the boys to take their plates to the sink while the girls quickly cleared the table and Rachel rinsed the dishes. TJ came along side her and asked about baths for the boys. Rachel wanted to establish a routine with them right away but was sensitive to the fact that they might need things to go slowly. She wasn't sure if they should push for too much on their first night.

"I got it, Rache," TJ assured her. They had talked before about some of the struggles kids that had been abused often had with bathing and even bathrooms in general.

"Hey, boys," he said to get their attention. "Thank Mama for supper and then we gotta get ready for bed."

Ben said a quiet thank you, for TJ's approval, Rachel was certain. But Ricky came over and gave her legs a big hug. She smiled at Ben and patted Ricky's head. "You're welcome, boys."

Remembering their suitcase and bag of things were still in the entry way, she asked the girls to finish up in the kitchen and went to get their belongings. Then she followed TJ and the boys.

"Ben, I have your bags here. Let's take them to your room so you can go through them and put them away."

TJ took the suitcase from her and set it on Ben's bed. Rachel stepped back so Ben could sort it. There were several shirts and pairs of pants, some shorts, underwear, mismatched socks and one pair of pajamas for each child but no toothbrushes or much of anything else for that matter. TJ caught her eye over the boys' heads. It was hard to imagine this was all they had.

"What's in the bag?" TJ asked.

"I show you!" Ricky ran over and dumped it. Out came two stuffed animals. Ricky quickly grabbed up one of them. There was a blanket for each boy, two Bibles and their toothbrushes. "This is our stuff we got from camp last summer!" Ricky said proudly.

Ben took his blanket, Bible and toothbrush. "These are mine," he said to no one in particular.

"Good job keeping track of your things!" Rachel praised him. "Um, you can wear your PJs you brought. Or if you want, there are new ones in your dressers. I will leave you guys to get ready." She smiled at the boys and leaned over to TJ. With a light kiss on the cheek, she left the room.

The boys took baths with no trouble at all. TJ leaned in the doorway then went in to wash their hair. He supervised their tooth brushing and gave them high fives for a job well done. When Rachel returned to say good night the boys were clean, sweet-smelling and wearing new PJs.

The girls wanted to say good night, too. They split up.

Gracie and Mary joined TJ in Ben's room and Rachel, Naomi and Emily went to say good night to Ricky. The small boy hugged Rachel's neck tightly. She had to gently unwrap his arms to tuck him in.

"Night, little guy," she whispered. "I am so glad you are here with us. Happy dreams, sweet boy." She switched on the small lamp atop the dresser and asked him if that would be okay. After telling him once more how near her room was and that Ben would be right next door, he seemed satisfied. Rachel asked if he would like the door open or closed.

"Open, please," he said and snuggled into his covers.

Rachel found Ben much less demonstrative in his affection. He did smile at her and the girls. She smiled back and adjusted his bedding so he could snuggle into the covers. She handed him his teddy bear and lightly lifted his hair back from his forehead. "Night, sweet angel-boy."

"Night," he said simply with no emotion.

She reminded him that her room was close by if he needed anything. He said he wanted his door mostly closed but liked the night-light she turned on.

Rachel, TJ and the girls met in the family room. The girls were beaming and TJ looked as if he had just won the lottery. He hugged his wife excitedly. "Shall we call Beth and Hope to tell them the boys have come?" he asked.

"Already texting Beth, Dad," Naomi said, deftly pushing buttons on her cell phone.

"Can I call Hope?" Emily asked.

"Go ahead, and make sure you let everyone get a chance to talk."

While the girls were telling their sisters about the boys, TJ and Rachel talked softly about the evening and their impressions. TJ commented on Ben's attitude. "He sure was more standoffish than I have ever seen him before," he observed.

"Well, back then we weren't a new family that might reject him," Rachel said thoughtfully. "Still, I think it falls in the normal range of what we should expect."

She thought about how happy TJ looked when Ben first saw his room. Her heart swelled at the tenderness with which he led the boys through the evening routine. "You were so amazing," she told him. "I have always loved watching you with kids. But tonight, especially with Ben, you were just incredible."

He laughed. "I don't know about that, but thanks, Babe." He kissed her.

She could feel the tension leaving as she leaned in his arms. She gave a contented sigh then thought about the boys waking up in a new house and Ben having to go to school as if nothing had changed. "Tomorrow should be interesting," she noted.

chapter

Rachel had heard that sometimes there was a honeymoon period when children came into a new home, a time of calm when they tried to put their best foot forward, maybe consciously or unconsciously, to convince the family to keep them. This was not going to be the case with Ben. From the moment he woke he seemed dead set on convincing them he did not want to be there and could care less if they wanted him.

Maybe that was exactly the point, Rachel thought as she watched him stomp around disgruntled that first morning. First he was mad they had awakened him. Then he was angry when he found out he had to go to school but Ricky didn't. He was furious because Rachel unwittingly moved his backpack. She told him she had done so to put his lunch into it but he didn't acknowledge that at all. He grabbed it from her hand and said, "Don't touch my stuff!" When he found out they had to drive over half an hour to get to his old school, he was incensed.

"The only good part about living here," he shouted at everyone in the kitchen, "is at least I get to still go to my real school with my real teachers and my real friends!"

TJ told him to get his backpack and go to the truck. He did it, but he stomped indignantly the whole way to the garage. At the door, Rachel smiled and told him to have a good day. He didn't answer. TJ gave her a hug. "Pray for me," he said. "I hope the whole car ride won't be like this."

"He is just nervous," Rachel reminded him. Then jokingly she added, "And you aren't the one that touched his backpack so maybe you are still the good guy here." She kissed his cheek and whispered in his ear, "Yes, we'll pray."

Rachel returned to the kitchen where Emily, Gracie and Mary were getting ready to head to school. TJ and Ben had not been gone long when Ricky came running from his room, hair ruffled and sleep lingering in his baby blue eyes. He looked around then ran into the family room. He continued racing from room to room. Rachel finally caught him as he headed upstairs.

"What are you looking for, sweet boy?" she asked.

"Where's my brother?" he demanded.

"He had to go to school today. You didn't have to go so we let you sleep a little longer."

Ricky looked up at her frantically. His eyes filled with tears. He sat on the bottom step, hands on his head and chin against his chest. He began sobbing. Rachel watched for a moment then sat next to him and put her arm around him.

"Ricky, he'll be back. He is with TJ. He is coming back."

"But—I—go—too," he choked out between sobs.

"Since this is your first day here we thought you might like to explore the house all by yourself." She craned her neck to see his face, but he hid it, inconsolable. So she just held him as he cried. She had seen this kind of emotion at camp from kids who were deeply wounded. The children she worked with often seemed very strong and stoic because of all they had been through. Many of them showed very little emotion. But when they did cry it seemed to come from some locked away place and the cries were much more intense than the moment dictated. Ricky's crying reminded her of that unfathomable pain and she felt her own heart breaking.

Rachel was glad he was able to cry. He must be feeling somewhat safe with her to let those tears out. Tears on the outside, meant healing on the inside. She comforted herself with the words she often told her clients. Gently, she pulled the boy closer. He allowed himself to be moved so that she had him completely in her arms. He didn't resist, but instead leaned against her.

Gradually, the sobs subsided. His body still convulsed occasionally. She thought of a song he might have heard at camp. It was called "Jesus' Love." She sang it softly and gently stroked his hair. Ricky put his thumb in his mouth and they sat together while Rachel rocked him. Finally, he drew a deep breath and sighed.

She finished the song. She thought he might have fallen asleep, but he opened his eyes and found her face. "Again," he said, thumb still in his mouth. So she sang through it once more. Then she moved him a little so he was sitting up. He looked at her intently and touched her cheek.

"Mama?" he asked her.

"Yes, Baby. I am your mama now. This is your home. We love you. You and Ben will live here from now on."

He didn't say anything. Rachel wondered what was going through his mind.

"Eat now?" he asked. "Tummy hungry!"

Rachel laughed. "Let me listen." She gathered him into her lap and put her ear on his tummy, pretending it was talking to her. "Yep, you are right. Tummy says, 'Hey lady, feed this kid!'"

Ricky giggled. He jumped off her lap and Rachel asked him if he remembered where the kitchen was. He took her hand. Together they walked down the hall. Rachel pointed him toward the bathroom to wash up while she went to get his breakfast ready.

The girls had left and Ricky was finishing his breakfast when TJ called.

"How did your drive go?" Rachel asked.

"Well, he settled down a little once we got going. The middle part was pretty good. We talked about playing catch with his new football when we got home. But as we got close to the school, back in his old neighborhood, you could see him start to tense up. Damn it, Rachel, I wish they would let us just take him home and start next year with his new school."

"I know. I think that would be best, too. But Social Services need to know we are going to comply with their requirements. At least that is how Lori explained it to me. So what happened?"

"His sour mood came back. He asked me, 'So do you think you are my dad now?' And I told him we were his family and I cared about him. I said we were all really glad he and Ricky were part of our family."

Rachel murmured in agreement.

"When that wasn't getting the reaction he wanted he asked me if he had to do what I said. I told him I knew it was difficult to suddenly change homes and rules and told him again we were glad he was here and we really wanted him to be part of our family."

"That's good, TJ. Sounds like you did great reassuring him despite his mood."

"Well, he pretty much sat there scowling. I have never seen him like this before. He has had a little temper with the other kids at camp, but this is—I don't know. If you hadn't warned me about this kind of stuff I would have thought we got the wrong kid. Anyway, he didn't say much as we drove into the drop-off area. Just grabbed his stuff and got out. As he left I told him I would be back to pick him up after school. No comment from him. He just gave me a hard stare and slammed the door. For a little guy he sure acted a lot like a teenager." TJ tried to laugh.

"Well, he has been through enough. Sounds like you did great though. How are you holding up?"

"I'm okay." TJ took a deep breath. "He reminds me of me

when I would go to school looking for a fight. Back then someone was going to pay for all the crap going on inside me."

"Yeah. Well, we know he has had plenty of trouble this year at that school."

"Poor kid, though. If one of us had just moved—which also means he just lost the family he had been living with the past four months—or if we had all the upheaval he has had in his short life, we would at least have the option of calling in sick. Probably any adult would take time off to mourn, to readjust, or to get settled. But not kids. They don't give kids a chance to catch up. Why is that, Rachel? Why do they expect kids to do business as usual? 'Go to school, turn in your homework. Oh, you moved into a new house and left it at your old house? Too bad. Stay in at recess then.'" Rachel could hear the frustration in TJ's voice. They had had this conversation before. They had even had it with Lori but had agreed to comply in the end. So despite better judgment and logic, Ben was at school the day after moving to a completely new family.

"It's because kids are resilient, TJ." she answered sarcastically. She'd heard it so many times and the idea irritated her immensely. With all the information on trauma and how it affected the brain and even created learning difficulties for kids, there was still little practical application or understanding from educators and others that worked with kids. "When we get further into this process hopefully we will have a lot more input at his school next year."

TJ's call waiting beeped.

"Uh-oh, Rache, the school is calling. Let me get this. I'll call you back."

Rachel hung up and began silently praying for her husband and for Ben. Meanwhile, Ricky had three helpings of eggs and two pieces of toast. She wondered if he was stashing it somewhere. He didn't look big enough to eat that much. She didn't see any place in his pajamas where he could hoard the food. She had read about kids growing several inches once they got into stable home environments. She wondered if that would happen with Ricky and Ben.

She directed him to take his plate and fork to the sink then asked him to wash his hands and get dressed for the day. "Do you want me to help you find some play clothes or can you do it?" she asked.

"I can do it."

He went down the hall while she straightened the kitchen. He was back shortly wearing his new wranglers; a cowboy shirt buttoned all wrong and his new boots. "Can we see horses?" he asked.

"That would great, but you gotta let me get ready, too." She looked at his shirt and asked if she could re-button it for him. He moved forward so she could fix it. When she was done, she tucked it in. "By the way, do you have socks on inside those boots?"

He guiltily shook his head. She sent him back to his room for socks. He reappeared, socks in hand. She explained that they wore shoes and boots only outside and removed them to be in the house, but she helped him get the socks on and put his boots by the garage door.

"Ricky, you can go in the TV room and watch a show, or you can play in your room while I get ready." He ran to his room, grabbed his bear and ran back to the TV room. In fact, he seemed to run wherever he went, Rachel observed humorously.

"Okay, how about Sesame Street?"

As she was finding the right channel, her phone rang. It was TJ. Ricky settled in to watch and Rachel went to her room to talk privately.

"Well, good thing I was staying close by today." TJ started right in. "Apparently he punched a kid as soon as they got into the classroom." Rachel sucked in her breath. She wasn't totally surprised but still she had hoped. "He is waiting in the office. I guess we're coming home early." TJ paused. "I have to go talk to the principal and the teacher. Do you want to come down here and make your case for just pulling him out? Do you think I should call Lori?"

"Oh, boy," Rachel sighed. "I'll put in a call to Lori. Don't go in there just yet. Let me call her first. I don't think I can come down. I really don't see that helping much, plus Ricky is doing well and I don't want to throw him off by taking him back to the old neighborhood. Let me call you back."

Rachel punched the cell number she had for Lori and told her about Ben's morning.

"Do you want to meet Troy down there and talk to the principal?" Rachel asked.

"I can't. I have a meeting in five minutes. But I will call the school when I'm done and call you back later today."

Rachel relayed the message to TJ. "Lori can't come to the school but she said to go ahead and take Ben home and she'll call the school later. But I think you should run an errand or two for me first."

"What? Now?"

"I think Ben needs to sit in the office for a bit. It's not okay that he hits someone and then we come rushing in to rescue him. And we both know we aren't going to punish him for this today. So just have him wait. He is safe there in the principal's office. Besides, I really do need you to get some stuff for me." She ended with a short laugh, trying to lighten the mood.

"That makes sense I guess. You're the expert. So what do you need from the store?"

Rachel gave him a short list and figured he would run the errands, meet with the principal and be home in a couple of hours.

Meanwhile, she knew Ricky was waiting eagerly to go see horses. She got ready and pulled on an old ball cap. Ricky wore his real cowboy hat. Together they put on their boots.

The horses grazed out in the field near the newer barn. Rachel kept the ones she used for therapy with the kids close to the barn and arena. They had been built before Rachel knew TJ, but since she used them the most they had become hers. The arena was covered so her clients were able to work with the horses all year round. Some of the work in the summer was what she called "horse time," allowing kids to come and ride. But a lot of the therapy was done without riding.

She loved working with families in the arena. It was a powerful tool Rachel likened to art therapy. Naomi, Gracie, Emily and Mary helped during the summer with kids that came to ride.

Ricky had met all the horses before. He was bouncing around, impatient to get going.

Rachel backed the Ranger out of the garage. Similar to a four-wheeler except with a small pickup-type bed in back, the Ranger was great for farm chores. The older kids loved using it to help feed the horses. In the old barn at the end of the road TJ had a tractor that Buck, his hired hand, used. There was also an old truck TJ liked to tinker with when he had time. The old barn had plenty of memories. Though she didn't get out there much Rachel loved it. That was where TJ proposed to her so, of course, it had special meaning. Last year, he had taken her down there on the anniversary of the proposal.

When he had first asked her to marry him she hadn't said yes right away. He reminded her of that fact and said he wanted to right that wrong. So he asked her to marry him again and this time she said yes in a heartbeat. They lingered there in the moonlight for some time.

She and Ricky headed down the driveway to find Bob, Tracker, Shy Girl and Missy, all horses the boy claimed as his favorites. Maverick and Lady ran alongside the Ranger. As they drove, Ricky asked her if she was a real cowboy.

"Well, I got boots, don't I?"

"Yeah, but are you a real cowboy?"

"Well, I am a girl, not a boy, but I have horses."

"Yes, but are you a really real cowb—girl?"

"I can ride and I have a real hat like yours. I don't know, Ricky, am I a real cowgirl?"

He looked at her pensively. "Okay," he nodded in firm agreement. "I guess you are a really real cowgirl."

She didn't know what was going on in his head but having that settled, he seemed content. "I guess that makes you my little buckaroo," she grinned.

He looked at her questioningly.

"A buckaroo is the cowboy's helper. He's a cowboy, too, but still learning."

"Okay." He smiled and took her hand. "I am your buckaroo."

When they got to the barn they each took a rake and cleaned part of the pen where the horses were. It was a farm rule—work first, then play. They got carrots out of the small fridge in the barn, collected Shy Girl's pony-sized halter and went into the field to call the horses.

By the time TJ and Ben got home Rachel and Ricky had finished up and were casually eating lunch. Rachel heard the car pull up and held her breath as she waited to see what kind of mood would come walking through the door. Ricky's happy chatter stopped when he heard the door close behind TJ. He jumped off his chair and ran to his brother.

Ricky gave Ben a warm hug and an enthusiastic hello. They were not returned. Undeterred, Ricky next made a bee-line for TJ. Seeing him coming, TJ knelt to welcome him and scooped him up in his arms.

"Hi, little man." TJ straightened up holding Rick and gave Rachel a nod toward Ben. Rachel understood he was giving her some time with the older boy. She told him Ricky had been eating lunch and he headed toward the kitchen. She stepped into the hallway toward Ben.

His face was dirty and his hair disheveled. For the moment it looked as if all the fight had gone out of him. In his eyes Rachel once again saw the strange paradox of a very young boy and a much older child, one who already knew more than he should about the hardships of life. She could see he was being brave but inside he must have been wondering about punishment.

Rachel wanted to hug him and tell him it was going to be okay. She longed to hold him like she had Ricky earlier. But she knew he wouldn't let himself be comforted in that way. Instead, she motioned for him to follow her to his room. He sat on the bed and looked up at her then quickly looked down at his hands. She wasn't sure how the principal's office had gone or what TJ had said to him on the way home or even what the fight had been about. All she saw was a very hurt six-year-old with more questions and fears than any kid should have to carry.

"Ben—"

He looked toward her. His defiance was gone. She saw fear

in his eyes.

She gave him a small smile and said tenderly, "Looks like you had a tough day. Do you want to tell me about it?"

He shook his head and lowered his gaze again. His body tensed as if waiting for a blow to come. She watched him pick at his fingernail.

"Did you eat your lunch yet?"

He shook his head.

"Me neither," she said. "Why don't you go wash your hands, pull the lunch out of your backpack and come join us in the kitchen."

Ben looked up, surprised. "Yes, ma'am."

She smiled warmly and lightly touched his shoulder as she turned to leave. Walking to the kitchen, she prayed inwardly for Ben and hoped today in some small way they could set his troubled heart at ease.

Though Ricky had finished his lunch, he sat at the table with his brother excitedly filling him in on his work as a buckaroo. Ben gobbled his food not saying much though he seemed to be taking in everything Ricky was telling him. After lunch Rachel instructed both boys to go to their rooms for a quiet time. She was pretty sure Ricky would take a nap but she was right in thinking Ben would resist the idea of lying down. He growled under his breath, saying he wasn't a baby and didn't need a "stupid nap." When he tried to walk past her to his room, Rachel placed her hand on his shoulder and told him she didn't expect him to take a nap.

"Just play quietly in your room and let Ricky sleep," she said gently.

He pulled away from her touch and walked defiantly down the hall. Rachel looked over at TJ who was watching the whole scene.

"Let him go, Babe. I can't tell you how much he is reminding me of myself." He shook his head. "Poor kid."

TJ took Rachel's hand and led her into the living room, filling her in on what the principal had said about Ben and follow-up disciplinary actions. "Basically, the school would be fine with us pulling him for the rest of the year. The last couple months, he has bitten two kids and pushed or hit several more. We aren't part of his educational team and it is too late in the year to rewrite his IEP (individual educational plan). They know we aren't bringing him back there next year. Frankly, Rachel, they seem relieved he might not be back."

Rachel nodded. She had heard as much herself when she tried to meet with school officials a couple of weeks earlier. She asked TJ for Ben's side of today's fight.

"He told me in the car he didn't hit anyone. He said he just 'pushed a kid that was being a jerk.' Piecing together what he said and what the teacher said, his push came with a punch that knocked the boy backward hard enough to bang his head pretty good." TJ shook his head again.

"So how did it go on the way home?"

"Well, he was pretty worried, you could tell. Probably thought I was going to yell at him or worse. He sat as close to the window and as far away from me as he could. He looked so small, Rache. I can't be mad him right now. I am more upset that anyone expected him to go to school today when everything in his life has changed again." TJ fiddled with his ring. "I told him I used to fight a lot in school, too. I told him I understood he had a lot of stuff to deal with and we would talk about fighting and all that later. Then I put the radio on low and he actually slept the rest of the way home."

Rachel felt tears come to her eyes. She thought about all the things she knew Ben had already experienced in his short life. She tried to imagine TJ at that age but kept seeing Ben instead. She reached over and took TJ's hand.

"You doing okay?"

"Yeah. I just—" He shook his head and pulled Rachel close to him. They were silent for a moment. Then TJ asked, "Do you think he should have consequences for today?"

"I was thinking about that, about what Lori might say, or the school. But then I think about what needs to happen here so he can trust and heal. I don't know, TJ. But I think we gotta rely on our instincts. God gave these boys to us and He will show us how to love them and how to raise them. I know the school and Social Services might say he needs to be punished in some way but my gut says no, not this time. We need to pull him close. He wants to see if we will send him away."

"What did Lori say when you talked to her?" TJ asked.

"She hasn't called me back yet. But she knew you were bringing him home. I think Lori will back us up. What do you think we should do the rest of the day once the boys are up?"

"We have Emily's and Gracie's softball game tonight. You'll have the boys while I am busy coaching. Do you need me to take the guys this afternoon so you can do whatever you need to do? Or do you want to do something together?"

"I have today cleared and I can get some things done now while they are resting. Let's take the boys out to the pond. It would be good to just let them wear themselves out a bit before the game. Do you know if the school is expecting Ben tomorrow?"

"I told them I would gladly keep him home but they want to talk to Lori about it. Since we just got Ben they see Lori as the final authority on what happens right now. They don't normally expel kindergarteners is what they told me." He chuckled. "I think they told my mom something like that when

I was about eight. My God, Rachel, do you think God's got a sense of humor?"

"What, you mean by giving you a son just like you?" She smiled at him. "No doubt." Then she kissed him soundly. Coming up for air she added, "Ben may not know it but he couldn't have a better daddy."

chapter

The Little Boy

He was running hard and fighting harder. Streams of sweat soaked the back of his shirt and ran down his face. No matter how hard he fought he couldn't stop the beatings and his terrified soul gave him no comfort even when he slept. He swung his arms wildly trying to land a punch. It was useless. He was useless. Still Troy fought. Even in his sleep he fought.

"Stop, damn it!" he yelled. Thrashing violently, he kicked off sheets and blankets. He almost hit his sister. She stood by the bed to help him calm down. Troy finally opened his eyes and tried to focus on what was real and what was part of the terror that filled his dreams. Julie, six years old, stretched her small, soft hand to him and spoke tenderly. She told him it would be okay but her own eyes were wide. She hated his nightmares and she was always glad when he finally woke up.

"I'm okay, I'm okay," Troy said finally. His breathing was starting to slow but his heart still pounded. He could feel it in his ears. "Go back to bed, Sis." He was eight years old. By day, he was her protector and watchman. But at night, when the bad dreams overtook him, it was Julie that watched over him and comforted him. Their mom was usually gone during those times, working the night shift to make ends meet.

"Are you sure, Troy? Do you want a drink of water?" He would have said no, but she already held it out to him. He took a quick drink and tried to give her what he hoped was a reassuring smile.

"Thanks, Sis. I'm okay," he repeated. And he watched her crawl back into her bed on the other side of the room. He ran the back of his hand over his mouth and across his brow. He reached down and pulled his covers over his skinny frame. When his head hit the pillow he turned away from his sister and let tears flow silently.

It had been a year since George had been hauled away by the police. Their mom moved them to a smaller house closer to their grandparents. Even though the beatings had stopped Troy couldn't shake the fear and shame that lingered in his heart and overtook his dreams. At school he was fine. At least he felt fine. School was easy. He had lots of friends and he loved to play hard. Despite never really trying, he got good grades. Sure, sometimes he got into fights but only when the other kid really deserved it. Often when he fought and sometimes even when he played Troy felt anger bulging inside him. It rolled through him building like thunder cells growing into a big storm. The anger helped him run faster and hit harder but it also scared him.

Just yesterday some kid made a smart remark about Troy's sister as she stood nearby watching the boys play football. Troy warned him to shut up and leave her alone. But the kid didn't stop. He asked Troy if he was her babysitter and then made a few comments about their mother. Troy hit him hard in the mouth before he even finished his sentence. The boy dropped on the first punch, but the anger Troy felt was so strong he kept swinging even while the boy was on the ground. Troy's friend had to pull him back. The little wimp on the ground scrambled up and went running. Then, of course, Troy was in the office—again. His mom having to come to the school was bad enough but worse was the dreams that followed—bad dreams—almost as though a beast inside him had awakened, and all the memories.

He lay there in the dark and cried. Those were the only times he ever cried. He never cried taking a punch, not even when he broke his arm. But the memory of the helpless shame he felt watching his mom being hit by George and the man's taunting face overwhelmed him some nights. There was a box deep in his heart that held the names George called him, the mocking laugh and way he felt forever small and insignificant. He did his best to keep the box locked up tight but at night— Wiping tears from his face and taking a deep breath he promised himself he would never be that small again. If it meant beating up a thousand boys he would never stand by and watch his mom or his sister get hurt by some stupid jerk with a foul mouth.

chapter

That afternoon the boys were in the gym downstairs with TJ when Lori called. She asked Rachel how Ben was doing and what Ricky's day had been like. Rachel told Lori they would head out for a softball game when the girls got home. She sorted mentally through the events of the day, trying to decide what to tell the social worker.

They had taken the boys fishing at the pond earlier until they grew bored and wanted TJ to show them how to skip rocks across the water. Once Ben got frustrated with that, they had moved on, playing in the sand along the shoreline. They had seemed like two very normal, happy little boys until it was time to head back. Ricky whined about having to leave but Ben came completely undone and proceeded to throw a tantrum. Once Ben started in that direction, Ricky gave up and complied easily. Rachel found it interesting that when Ben was acting out Ricky did whatever it took to show he was being good.

TJ firmly told Ben he could complain all he wanted but they had to go. Ben picked up a good-sized rock as if to throw it at TJ. The man reached over and deftly knocked it out of his hand much like a basketball player stealing a ball. He never touched Ben as he neutralized the immediate threat. Ben kicked the dirt and yelled obscenities. TJ motioned for Rachel to come.

"Ben, I know you are having fun out here and you don't want to leave," he said, "but we have more fun stuff to do today. Now you can get in the Ranger and ride back with us or I will take Ricky back and you and Mama can walk back together. If you don't walk nicely with her she will have to hold onto you. I don't have any more time to wait. So I am going to get the stuff in the Ranger. I will give you a minute to decide and then you will be walking. Is that okay with you, Mama?"

Rachel nodded agreement. Years earlier in her training

Rachel had worked in a psychiatric hospital with adolescents. She had learned how to escort unwilling patients with confidence and had on occasion used that knowledge with troubled children. Still, she was relieved when Ben sullenly shuffled over to the Ranger and climbed into the back to ride with Ricky rather than choosing to be escorted up the long hill back to the house. She figured Ben knew TJ was serious.

"Good choice," TJ said once he was settled in the Ranger.

Rachel decided to tell Lori about the difficult transition at the pond, about her morning with Ricky and about the mood Ben had started his day with. Rachel asked if he couldn't at least have the rest of the week off to settle in and become a little more comfortable with his new surroundings. "I know you are worried about setting a pattern with him where we rescue him when he gets in trouble, but I can almost guarantee you if he has to go to school again tomorrow he will do something else that will put him right back here anyway," Rachel argued. "I think he just needs to stay close to Ricky and to us right now. That's my personal and my professional opinion."

Lori had already talked to the school. The principal wanted to keep Ben out for the remainder of the year because so many parents had complained about his aggressive behavior. Legally, they couldn't kick him out since he was on an IEP that dictated social skills as part of his special needs. Lori was sympathetic.

"You know I agree with you Rachel. I do trust your instincts with this boy. I can let you guys keep him out this week. But Monday morning, come hell or high water, he has to be back in that classroom."

"Good enough," Rachel conceded. "Maybe we will send TJ as his personal aide on Monday."

"Not a bad idea. I've recommended a paraprofessional for

him several times, but with budget cuts and other kids with greater needs, that fell on deaf ears."

"Lori, what if he really hurts someone badly? Then what? And one other thing—do you think Ricky is in danger? Should we be cautious here at home?"

"There have been no reports of him hurting Ricky. He is very protective of his family. We do know that Ben seems to do better when he and Ricky are in the same home. We had them separated for a couple months last year and both kids had increased problems. I have a lot of hope for these boys, Rachel. Ben is smart and he has an incredibly tender side. We are really pulling for you down here. I know the red tape makes it seem we don't care but we want this to work as much as you do."

Rachel thanked her before she hung up. As she finished packing dinner for the family to eat at the game she rejoiced that they didn't have to send Ben to school tomorrow for a repeat performance. She wondered what the rest of the week would hold for them and prayed for wisdom as they worked to build trust and stability.

That night after the boys were asleep and the girls were upstairs Rachel fell into bed, exhausted. TJ put his arms around her and whispered in her ear. "Hey, Mama, how are you holding up?"

She turned toward him, touching his cheek tenderly and looking into the love and warmth of his eyes. "I'm doing okay. Lots of emotions. And I'm tired. But I had a good day with Ricky. He asked me if I was his mama. That was pretty much a Hallmark moment. He is really sweet."

TJ took her hand and brought it his lips, kissing her fingers.

"What do you think we should do tomorrow since we have the rest of the week?" Rachel asked.

"Hmm. I don't know. Simple things." TJ smiled at her.

"Kind of like what I want." He caressed her fingertips with his lips. She knew what he wanted.

"Simple?" She raised her eyebrows. "I thought you knew enough about women to know there is nothing simple about loving a woman. It is complicated, Babe, very complicated."

He gave a short chuckle as he moved closer to kiss her mouth.

"I'd better get started then," he teased. His lips met hers. She wrapped her arms around his neck and returned his kiss.

"I love you," she said simply. For the moment, it was just the two of them lost in their love and passion. Rachel loved the way he enfolded her and how their hearts beat as one. From the inside out, Rachel thought. That was their love and their life.

She fell asleep with her head on his chest and his arms around her. She thought she heard something. It awakened her. The digital clock by the bed read two a.m. In her foggy sleep state she couldn't at first identify the noise. Her girls had long passed those early years of bad dreams and restless nights. She had almost forgotten the sounds of small children crying in the darkness.

She quickly put on her robe. It was coming from Ben's room.

Ricky surprised her at Ben's door. "Bad dreams," he whispered. "Benny has bad dreams."

Rachel touched his head and told him she would help Ben. "You go back to bed, sweetie." But Ricky followed her into the room.

Ben had kicked his blankets off the bed. In his sleep he looked as if he were fighting someone or something. Rachel could see he was sweating and he whimpered something indiscernible. She looked back at Ricky and then went over to the bed. None of her girls had ever had night terrors but the kids at the overnight camp for abused children frequently did. Rachel knelt and prayed before she spoke quietly, hoping to sooth him.

"It's okay, honey. Mama's here." She didn't want to wake him too quickly. She spoke softly. She thought about touching him gently but decided against it. "Shhh, sweet boy. It's okay." He cried out in his sleep and jerked violently. Rachel prayed again.

He came fully awake with a start, sitting straight up. He looked directly at Rachel, but he didn't appear to know who she was or where he was. He looked wildly around the room then back at her. He was slowly regaining his bearings.

She smiled and touched his arm. "Hey," she said quietly. "It's okay. You're okay."

He was breathing hard but allowed her to sooth him. He looked past her and noticed Ricky. Seeing his little brother's worried look, he tried to be brave and pull himself together for the younger boy.

"I'm okay." He repeated her words, nodding toward Ricky. Rachel moved his hair off his damp forehead. Slowly he eased back on his bed. "I'm okay," he said again, this time mostly to himself.

Rachel sang "Jesus' Love" softly and he closed his eyes. His breathing quieted. His body gradually calmed until finally he slept. She kissed his cheek and carefully pulled the covers over him. "Night, my little angel-boy." She had heard that abused children often had a much faster resting heart rate than normal and she wondered about this as she watched him. Before leaving she again whispered a prayer.

When she turned TJ stood in the doorway with Ricky in his arms. She hadn't heard him come in.

"Bad dream," she said.

"That's what I heard."

Together they put Ricky back in bed and prayed with him that he would have a good sleep. Back in their room Rachel told TJ about Ben's nightmare.

"I used to have bad dreams like that," he told her. "Almost every time, after fighting it would happen. Even when I got older if something made me really angry I would have horrible dreams about my stepdad hitting me or my mother." TJ paused. Even in the dimly lit room Rachel could tell the memories were still vivid. His face held traces of the pain from those times. "My mom worked nights so Julie was the only one that knew about the nightmares. I didn't think much about them during the day. A lot of times I didn't even remember having them. When we moved close to my grandparents I stopped getting into so many fights and the nights were better." He sighed heavily.

Rachel encouraged him to continue. He had never told her about the nightmares before.

"When I got married the dreams came back and actually got worse. Kris was really worried about me, about how violent the dreams were I think. Drinking helped actually but that wasn't exactly working for Kris and me." He gave a sad chuckle. "That was when I went into counseling. The therapist helped me talk about all the abuse and finally getting it all out helped with the dreams. They were tied together." He shook his head. "Hadn't really thought about it since then until I saw you with Ben tonight."

"I'm sure it is all connected with Ben, too."

"Yeah." TJ was quiet.

Rachel thought about both boys, Troy as a scared little guy and also the one sleeping across the hall.

When TJ spoke again it was soft and tender. "Rachel, you

keep telling me how lucky those boys are to have me as their dad, but Rache, you are such an amazing mama. And I am so glad we have you—me, the boys, all of us." He wrapped her in his arms. They fell asleep tucked together.

chapter

The week with the boys at home taught Rachel a great deal more about Ricky and Ben. She was glad to have the time to get to know them better and to set into place some general routines. They had been right about Ben needing time to just be with his brother and his new family. Both boys had issues and worries from years of never knowing if their basic needs would be met. Consistency was a simple thing the family could offer and both boys were starving for it.

The routines included regular meals and sleeping schedules, when to wake and when to sleep. Ben and Ricky needed constant attention and supervision. Even something as simple as having enough food was not a given in their former lives. Both boys ate each meal as if it were their last. More than once Rachel or TJ had to stop them from hiding food in their pockets. Rachel had read about kids that ate so much when they first went to homes with plenty of food that unless their intake was limited they would make themselves sick. So far the boys hadn't gorged to that point but they did eat a lot and try to stock up in case another meal wasn't around the corner. Rachel was always surprised when they were hungry and eager for the next meal or snack.

For the most part Ben continued to be fiercely independent and resistant to affection or help. Throughout the week he pushed Rachel away in every way he could. While he would walk beside TJ and seemed to hold him in great esteem he was still aloof and almost untouchable to Rachel. She had to admire his resolve and her understanding of the skills necessary for abused children to cope helped her be patient. She knew it wasn't personal and kept in her mind that he was afraid of his neediness.

Rachel was no stranger to kids with attachment issues and their craving to control their environments. She knew she and

TJ must work together so he couldn't play them against one another. During the day, as much as possible, he would avoid asking anyone to help, especially Rachel. In fact, he would talk to her only when absolutely necessary. Several times Rachel caught him studying her, sizing her up.

She and TJ had worked it out that he would have to interact with her to get things he wanted or needed. Both of them had seen these behaviors in other kids at one time or another but they had never had their skills tested so thoroughly in their own home. At times Rachel doubted if she had the strength, character or perseverance to parent these boys.

Thankfully, there were times of reprieve. At night, when he got sleepy, Rachel noticed Ben's defenses lower. She took full advantage and used the moments before bed to bond with him as much as he would allow. She was grateful for the small opportunity to end each day with a peace offering and loving good-night. He wasn't affectionate but he would let her sing to him softly. Even though he was such a tough guy, he seemed to like it when she called him angel-boy and tucked him in at night. At least he didn't push her away.

Ricky, on the hand, was loving and vivacious about everything and everyone. He would climb into the girls' laps so they could read to him. He gave Rachel numerous hugs throughout the day and seemed genuinely happy to be part of the family. He was willing to go wherever with whomever and do whatever. You couldn't help but smile at him as he easily captured the attention of everybody he met. He called Rachel Mama and TJ Daddy from the first day and seemed to love having big sisters. He set about to make everyone, animals and people, his best friends. Even Buck, the old ranch hand, who normally went about his business and didn't talk much, found Ricky compelling and allowed him to follow him around or ride on the tractor.

With such extremes in their personalities and attitudes about their new family it was surprising how close the brothers were to one another. If they hadn't insisted on doing just about everything together it would have been easy for Rachel to just allow TJ to take Ben to pal around with him while she and the girls spent time with Ricky. Of course, Rachel knew the distance Ben wanted to keep between them was more about his need to control the relationship and his own emotions than about her personally. And although he bordered on downright rudeness at times, she hung in there with him throughout his week at home, matching his aloofness with unconditional love and steady assurance. With the roller coaster ride of emotions and behaviors, Rachel was thankful TJ was home to help tag team when it seemed overwhelming.

Wednesday night after Ben's bad dream he seemed pretty mellow. So Thursday, TJ and Rachel decided to help the boys find the flow of the family by introducing some basic rules and routines. It was undoubtedly the calm before the storm. Friday morning was turbulent and went from bad to worse. Ben got up early and found his way to the kitchen where Rachel was putting dishes away from the night before and chatting with Emily, Mary and Gracie. He quietly surveyed the scene. The girls said good morning to him and he said hello. But when Rachel greeted him he physically turned away from her and asked where TJ was.

"He is out on his morning run," Rachel replied casually. "Do you want some breakfast?"

He didn't respond. Instead he walked deliberately to Gracie and asked if she could get him a bowl of cereal. Emily caught her mom's eye and raised an eyebrow. Rachel just nodded as if she expected this. Gracie started to get up from the table to get him a bowl but Rachel told her to go ahead and finish eating since she had to get going to school soon.

"Do you want some cereal?" Rachel asked Ben again. This time he turned and looked her in the eye defiantly.

"No."

She kept her eyes on his and didn't look away. "That would be, 'No thank-you.'" She prayed only love would show in her eyes.

His look hardened to a glare and he stomped out of the kitchen. "I hate you!" he yelled over his shoulder and slammed the door to his room.

Rachel sighed. The girls gave her questioning looks.

"What the heck?" Emily asked.

"He is a tortured soul," Rachel said lightly. "It's okay, girls. Better get going." She kissed and hugged each of them.

"Is he going to be alright?" Mary asked.

"Well, he may have a rough day. Yesterday was somewhat peaceful but today is a new day." She smiled cheerfully. "We will be alright, though. Besides, your dad is here if I need help. No worries, Hon."

Once the girls were gone Rachel sat at the table with her cup of coffee and prayed for wisdom and for love to guide her. She wanted to go to Ben's room to see if he would talk with her but decided against it. There was a moment of calm and she wanted to savor it. Somewhere deep inside she knew today was a day that would try her soul.

TJ came in, poured a cup of coffee, walked over to Rachel and kissed her cheek. He didn't get too close since he was sweaty from his run. "Good morning, beautiful." She smiled but he must have seen something in her eyes. "What? Did the girls get off okay?"

"They're all fine. Ben's up. I think he's drawing battle

plans for the day." She told him about their encounter.

TJ listened but Rachel could tell he was irritated. "Rache, I'm not going to be able to tolerate him being rude to you. You know this, right?"

"I don't think we have to tolerate rudeness, TJ. He can respond politely at the very least." She put her hand on his arm. "But you just need to understand, his battle with me isn't really about me. He is looking for places where he can gain some control."

TJ nodded.

Rachel added lightly, "I may need you to remind me of that if it starts getting to me, okay?"

"Will you tell me if it gets to be too much for you?" He was serious. "This isn't a fifty minute hour, you know. This is our life."

She knew what he was talking about. She had her own control issues to watch out for. She tended to pull away when things got hard. When she most needed to lean on him she was tempted to feel she had to figure things out on her own.

It was her turn to nod.

He kissed her again. "I'm going to see what he is doing and then take a shower. Sounds like Ben's breakfast today is all yours since he is so sure he doesn't need you." TJ gave a short chuckle and started toward the hall. "Guess when he gets hungry enough he'll call a truce."

"I hope so," Rachel replied.

"Well, I'm with you, Rache."

God, I love that man, Rachel thought putting her coffee mug in the sink. She prayed as she watched him go. In only a moment, he was back.

"Rache," he whispered quietly from the doorway.

She looked up. He motioned for her to follow him. Her

stomach churned. The look on his face made her immediately nervous. He softly opened the door to Ben's room.

It looked like a disaster zone. Every poster had been torn from the walls and lay shredded and scattered. His bedding was thrown on the floor in a heap. His new stuffed animals, once on the bed, looked as if they had been attacked by a wild animal. All the stuffing had been pulled out and thrown everywhere. Only the bear Ben had brought with him was unharmed. It sat safely on the dresser as if watching the show featuring Ben's rage. His clothes were out of their drawers and strewn about the room.

TJ looked at Rachel, incredulous. She shrugged her shoulders at him and shook her head. She had no idea such a small boy could do so much damage so quickly and quietly.

"What's going on?" TJ asked in his low voice.

Intent on his destruction, Ben hadn't heard them come in. At the sound of TJ's voice he jumped and stopped tearing the poster in his hand. At first Rachel saw fear in his eyes but then his startled look turned to rage again. His eyes narrowed. "I hate it here! I hate it here! I want to go home!" He shouted the words and finished tearing up what was left of the Titan's team picture.

Rachel looked at TJ but he kept his eyes on Ben. Then Ben looked away from TJ and noticed Rachel standing by the door. "I hate this house! You hate me! Let me go!" he shouted at her.

She prayed that love would pour through her to this boy, this hurt and frightened child.

"Ben." TJ spoke calmly but firmly. Ben looked at him, breathing hard, his small hands in tight fists. For a moment it seemed he might just stop with the sound of TJ's voice. But his pause didn't last long. Before TJ could say anything else, Ben grabbed his new football helmet and threw it against the wall, narrowly missing TJ's head.

The helmet made a huge crash and dented the wall. "Go away! I hate you!" he yelled.

TJ rubbed his chin. Rachel knew he was trying to keep his own emotions in check. She turned toward him and saw Ricky standing behind her. The noise must have awakened him. Ricky looked at her, his eyes full of fear and tears. She touched TJ's arm and moved so he could see Ricky standing there.

He drew a deep breath and let it out slowly. He stood still for a long moment then went over and picked up the smaller boy. "Good morning, Ricky. Did you just wake up?"

Ricky nodded and tears dropped from his cheeks.

"Rache, should we get Ricky some breakfast?"

TJ gazed at her. Rachel wasn't sure what he had in mind. She didn't want to leave either one of them alone with Ben. She looked questioningly and shook her head slightly as if to ask, "What?"

He continued, "I think we should let Ben finish up here and get Ricky some breakfast. Don't you think so, Mama?"

He jerked his head, signaling her to move toward the door and go along with him. He seemed to have a plan so Rachel decided to play along.

"Yep. You hungry, Ricky?" She patted the little boy on the back. He leaned over and put his arms tightly around her neck. She took him from TJ. They backed out of the room but stood by the doorway for a moment.

TJ stepped into the room and spoke resolutely to Ben. "You go ahead and finish what you need to do here, Son. When you're done we would like you to eat with us. I'm coming right back. I'll be back in a minute to see how you are doing." Then he turned and led Rachel and Ricky back to the kitchen.

Rachel tried to set Ricky in a chair but he clung to her.

"I don't want to leave," he cried into her neck.

She hugged him and then pulled his arms away from her neck. "Nobody is leaving."

TJ came and stood by her.

"Ricky, this is your home," TJ told him. "It's okay. You boys are staying. No one is leaving."

The boy studied them silently then swiped at his tears with the back of his hand. Rachel saw his shoulders visibly relax.

"Sweet boy," Rachel said, "Why don't you go wash up so you can eat. Do you want some cereal for breakfast?"

He nodded and jumped down from his chair, running down the hall to the bathroom.

Rachel gazed at TJ He looked as spent as she felt and it wasn't even nine a.m. yet. "Think he'll come out anytime soon?" she asked.

"I don't know. Not sure what happens next. Do you know?"

"I'm not writing this story," Rachel said. "We'll know soon enough."

Ricky came back and showed Rachel his clean hands. She put a bowl of cereal in front of him and kissed the top of his head. He looked up at her then turned and looked at TJ.

"Benny bad?" It was more a statement than a question.

"No, Baby. Benny's not bad," Rachel assured him. "We love Ben."

TJ nodded in agreement. He put his hand on Ricky's little shoulder. "I'm going to go see if he wants to eat with you."

"Can I come?" Ricky asked.

TJ hesitated. He and Rachel exchanged "what do you think" glances.

Rachel nodded. "Okay, little man."

TJ and Ricky set off toward Ben's room together. Rachel wanted more than anything to go with them and watch to see what would happen next. But she knew she needed to stay put and be as natural as possible. She exhaled, realizing she was holding her breath, waiting. She turned on the radio softly so she could listen as she absent-mindedly wiped the counters. TJ's number-one hit, "Faith and Family," was partway through. She sang along remembering the day she and the girls had gone to the studio with him to record it.

"God didn't promise days without pain," he sang.
Rachel listened to TJ's smooth, deep voice. The words resonated in her heart and soul.

Laughter without sorrow is like sun without rain,
But somehow we manage to get through the day
And faith guides our way.
He can calm even the roughest storm and change every little thing
Sometimes He calms the child within
And changes things unseen.
But He always gives enough strength for the day.

Rachel sang along on the chorus, the same part where their girls sang with him.

Hope, faith and love,
He gives us comfort for our tears,
Sunshine in the rain,
Family for love and joy in our pain.
When we start to unravel
His love helps us stay, strength for the day
And faith paves the way.

Rachel wiped tears from her eyes. TJ came into the kitchen as the song was ending. He smiled at her.

"That sounds familiar," he said lightly, moving closer to her. "The boys are getting their hands washed. I'm not sure what Ricky said to him but they worked out some sort of a deal. I decided to stay out of it." He whispered in her ear as the boys came in. "We'll talk with him later."

Rachel looked over at her two little guys. Ricky got up in his chair and picked up his spoon to eat his cereal. Ben stood still near the table. Rachel went over to him. He didn't look at her and she didn't demand that he do so.

"Would you like some cereal now, Ben?"

He nodded.

Rachel pulled his chair away from the table. "Great. Go ahead and have a seat." As he climbed into the chair and she turned to get him a bowl, Rachel let out a long breath and for the second time that day she was aware of holding her breath. She tried to let go of the tension she felt in her chest and shoulders.

Lori called Monday morning to find out how the weekend had gone. Rachel filled her in on some of the highs and lows. She told Lori about Ben's room episode and how later in the day TJ and Ben had worked together to clean it up and throw away the things he had ruined.

"He is definitely better with TJ than with me but even so, Lori, he is pushing as hard as he can. Do you think it's all about seeing if we are going to keep him?"

"Letting himself be loved is the greatest risk he can imagine. Sounds like he is laying it all on the line. He's one of those kids that is going to be as bad as he can right off the bat to see if you're going to get rid of him. He must really want to stay. How are you guys holding up?"

Rachel told her she and TJ were tired. It had been a long weekend but they had made it through. The other kids were also having their moments of struggle.

"Ricky's worried about being sent away along with Ben so he keeps trying to be as good as gold. We keep reassuring him.

The girls are disappointed to say the least that Ben ruined the room they worked so hard to create for him. Naomi is the only one that hasn't pulled back a little. The other girls have compassion but they aren't as understanding when he acts out. And they are probably worried to some extent about how it's affecting me."

Lori was encouraging. She was usually the one who called Rachel when she had problems with a family or with really tough kids. But Rachel liked having someone that knew the boys to bounce ideas off of.

"TJ's been pretty strict about the boys' manners," Rachel said, filling her in on how they were handling the issues. "We told Ben he could be angry but that we expected all the kids to at least be polite. How the girls talk to each other and to us has always been a big deal to TJ. Must be his southern upbringing." Rachel laughed. "Out west we have a higher tolerance for rudeness I think." Lori laughed along with her.

"TJ's always been adamant that one of his most important jobs as a daddy and a man is to teach the girls and now the boys how men should treat women," Rachel said seriously. "Other than insisting on that, we are doing what we can to avoid power struggles. Oh, and when they cleaned up the room together, Ben had to hand over all the objects they thought might be dangerous. His room looks pretty bare."

Rachel told Lori how Ben had cried and promised he would be good. "He likes having his own things but TJ held firm and told him it wasn't about being good, it was about being safe. He also let him know that once he was settled in he could get things back but he would have to earn them." She and Lori had talked about this strategy with troubled kids before.

"How did the rest of the weekend go?" Lori asked.

Rachel told her about going to the softball games and then

to the zoo on Saturday and to church on Sunday. "Except for a few minor things, it was fine. We knew it was going to be rough. They actually do alright when we are out and about, but at home Ben's fighting pretty hard to push me away. But I expected as much. When he gets tired, though, he has been letting me tuck him in bed. It's like he calls a truce at night." Rachel laughed. "He sure is a tough little boy."

Rachel was thankful for Lori and her heart for the boys as well as her trust in Rachel as a mother and a therapist. There were some caseworkers Rachel knew that seemed to have lost empathy and hope for the kids they worked with. It was understandable. Day after day they dealt with the most heartbreaking situations. Lori volunteered at one camp each summer and over the years she had referred literally hundreds of kids to camps, for therapy and mentoring programs Hope Enterprises had established.

As they were ending their conversation Lori shared an insight into Ben's and Ricky's souls that encouraged Rachel. "For foster children," she said, "it is impossible to love because they have not had love. And hope is just another word filled with disappointment. Having never belonged anywhere and believing no one really wants them, finding a home—a place to belong where the people won't give up on them, a place where their eyes match their words, and most importantly, a place to feel safe—is the primal need of their lives."

Lori's words resonated with Rachel's own heart as a former foster child, as a therapist working with troubled children, and now as a parent. She voiced her agreement. "I think the hardest part for kids like these is when they finally allow themselves to trust and find out they were only being used. It's going to be a long haul to remove the doubt."

"Don't give up, Rachel," Lori said. "I know you know how

scared those boys are. Call me if you need me to come over or call if you just need to talk through this stuff."

They said good-bye and Rachel went to check on Ricky. She hadn't heard anything from TJ yet about how Ben was doing at school. TJ planned to stay with Ben in the classroom. Rachel was praying they could make it through the rest of the school year without any more incidents.

She thought about their weekly family meeting the night before. It was the boys' first. Rachel could see that even Ben was proud to be a part. They met in the living room with Naomi, Gracie, and Mary on the couch, TJ on the floor by the boys and Rachel in the big oversized chair. Emily sat in the chair across from Rachel. They purposed to keep it short but wanted to get the boys started in this important ritual. Rachel asked Mary to explain what the family meetings were about and why they had them each week.

Mary said the most important reason was just to go over anything coming up the next week. Emily added that they also talked about the past week and made family decisions. Rachel was watching Ben. He looked around the room at all the faces. He appeared happier than she had seen him all week.

"Ben, do you want to start the meeting?" TJ asked. Ben's eyes grew wide at the possibility. "Start by telling us one high—something good this week—and one low or trouble this week. Do you want to?" Rachel thought he would decline but he surprised her and nodded.

"My good thing is coming here. My bad thing is being bad." He said it short and fast and without taking a breath. TJ put his hand on his shoulder and told him that was perfect.

Ricky was practically jumping up and down for the chance to go next. "Me! Daddy, me!"

"Okay, little man. Go ahead. What's your high?"

He threw up his arms and shouted, "Horses!" Everyone laughed at his enthusiasm.

"What's your low?" Mary asked.

Ricky's eyebrows knit together in concentration. His face suddenly became very serious. "Benny being mad." He said it quietly and looked down. Ben glared at him.

"Yep," TJ said. "That was tough." He patted Ricky's head. "Who else wants to go?"

Ricky moved over to Rachel and climbed into her lap. With his thumb in his mouth he watched everyone else share their highs and lows. Rachel played with his hair absentmindedly while she listened to the girls share.

Most of the meeting was about plans for graduations. Emily's and Gracie's high school was putting on a party they were intent on attending. Plus Emily would be singing at the ceremony. A week earlier, Beth would graduate from Ole' Miss and the family would travel with the Metcafes for Beth's and Laney's festivities.

The Keytons and Metcafes planned a big graduation party for both the high school and college grads. Tina and Rachel had been working on the details since long before the boys came. Rachel was always glad to get together with Tina and all the kids loved the chance to spend time with their "cousins," as they called the Metcafe girls.

TJ kept the meeting moving along and as short as possible. He wanted everyone to know what the plans were and to get the boys acquainted with the meeting process but he didn't want to wear them out by making it too long. It had been such a long weekend. Rachel could see it in TJ's face and feel it in her bones.

Nothing as dramatic as Friday morning had happened since, thankfully, but Rachel sensed constant tension from Ben as he fought hard to remain aloof. From where she sat, it was easy for her to study him. When he was calm like this, especially in the evenings when he started getting tired, it was difficult to imagine he could be so charged up and emotionally draining. She tried to imagine what was going on under the surface. Right now he looked like any other six-year-old.

He looked over at her and then his glance switched to his brother snuggled comfortably in her lap. He raised his eyes to hers and this time he focused on her. She smiled at him. His face showed no expression. He did not even return her smile. But Rachel saw a flicker of something in his eyes. It reminded her of the pain in TJ's eyes when she had first met him. He had been watching Mike and Tina's affection and Rachel saw the same look. It was loss, pain and longing. She realized it was in Ben's eyes watching Ricky cuddle up to her. She had seen that longing in numerous kids she had worked with.

Her heart went out to him because in that moment, as brief as it was, she saw a glimpse into his heart. She wished he understood he didn't have to protect himself. He could let down his guard. He really just wanted to know, from the inside out, that he was home.

For a moment, she thought he might come over and ask her to hold him, too. She prayed he would see the welcome in her eyes and heart.

chapter

The Little Girl

He was coming again. His heavy steps staggered down the hall. Rachel pretended to be asleep but her heart was pounding.

"Go to sleep! Go to sleep!" she told herself. But still her heart hammered in her chest. She heard the door open and then he was standing over her bed. Rachel held her breath. She could smell him. He smelled bad. It was the stuff he drank but it was more than that. His sweat repulsed her. That was the one thing she always thought of when he crawled into bed next to her. If his smell hadn't lingered so long after he was gone she might be able to convince herself that nothing happened. But as long as she lived Rachel would remember his scent.

She had learned to block out the memory of his touching and the slurred words. As she lay there pretending to sleep, she let her imagination take her far away.

Even though she was only five she knew she had to keep Mr. Wilcox's visits a secret. Besides, she didn't have anyone she could tell. Mr. Wilcox always made it seem she was part of the secret. Maybe it was her fault. Maybe he was right. Maybe if anyone found out she would be the one to get into trouble. So she went to school, played with friends and tried to fit in hoping no one would ever guess what her foster dad did to her in the middle of the night.

The real problem was he wasn't the only one that had touched her like that. Before foster care there had been her uncles and her mother's boyfriends. She didn't even remember the first time it happened. It was just the way it was.

Once she told a friend about it. That's when she found out what happened to her wasn't normal and it wasn't right. Her friend laughed and told her that was gross. Rachel didn't want to be weird or gross so she didn't talk about it to anyone anymore.

Deep inside Rachel felt bad, like a bad person. There had to be a reason for everything that happened. For Rachel that reason had to be something inside her that was wrong, different and made people use her or leave her. Maybe that was why her mom had left her, hated her it seemed, or why she wasn't allowed to be with her grandmother. Just like that Rachel had lost her whole family and been put here in this house with the Wilcoxes. A foster family, she was told. She had no idea where her brother was. No one ever explained anything to her. But maybe if she just did what they wanted and was really good she would get to go back to her family.

Besides, she told herself, there were things much worse than being touched and holding secrets. At least Mr. Wilcox didn't hit her. Rachel had been hit plenty—by her uncles, her aunts, her mother and now her foster mother. Before foster care her brother John had taken most of the hits and pushed her away to safety but he wasn't with her here. Now it was up to Rachel to figure out how to stay safe. For her that meant doing whatever they asked, not making them mad at her. Of course that was easier said than done. Her backside still stung from when Mrs. Wilcox spanked her to get her out of bed this morning.

Whenever Mrs. Wilcox was angry Rachel was afraid maybe she had found out about the secret. Always relieved that it wasn't that, Rachel didn't fight getting hit, being called stupid or lazy. She was just glad so far no one had said anything about the other stuff.

Even so, Rachel always felt worried—worried someone would find out about her, worried she didn't know as much as everyone else at school, worried she would be sent away again, and mostly worried she would be lost or forgotten.

Rachel also wondered where her brother was. He was a year older and her protector. Since they had been taken away from their house she had no idea where John was or when she would see him again. It wasn't like it was easy at her old house but she missed her brother and her grandmother. They were the only people Rachel knew that really cared about her.

Grandma always called Rachel her little girl. Grandma made clothes for her and was teaching her how to cook. It was crazy and fun at her house. She and John liked it better at Grandma's than being alone and hungry in their own house. At Grandma's there was always food and people around. Some of them were mean but at least there was plenty to eat at Grandmas and lots to do. Rachel missed being able to play and swim.

She tried to make friends, to laugh and be normal, but at five years old Rachel felt years older than her classmates. Her friends talked about what they would get for Christmas or their birthdays but Rachel wanted to talk about where her family was and if she would ever go back home. She was behind in school and felt stupid because she didn't know her ABC's or how to count like other kids. She tried to copy what others said and did. Just like she pretended everything was fine so no one would find out about Mr. Wilcox and what she let him do to her when he thought she was sleeping.

Above all, Rachel was afraid. She was deeply anxious that whatever it was about her that made her real mom hate her was the same thing Mrs. Wilcox hated about her. She was terrified that something inside her was terribly wrong. Why else would her mom leave her? Whatever that something wrong was, she had to keep others from finding out about it. For that reason, Rachel knew she had to try harder to be good and be normal. But in that hidden place where Rachel kept all the secrets she also knew it was highly unlikely she would ever be really wanted, truly loved or valued.

chapter

Rachel and TJ soon discovered Ben loved to go places and Ricky loved to stay home. When they went to Mississippi for the college graduation Ben was the model traveler. He sat in his booster seat without complaining, played games with the girls, begged for stories and asked Rachel and TJ questions about where they were going and what they would do. It helped that the SUV had a DVD player and he enjoyed movies. But even without the entertainment Rachel was amazed at how excited and relaxed he seemed the whole trip. This was the kid they had seen at camp, Rachel thought.

Ricky, on the other hand, was a little terror. He fussed and whined and begged to get out of his car seat. He whimpered all through the movies and couldn't get comfortable. When he did finally fall asleep he wet his pants. He cried to go home and see his horses and dogs. Ben was the only one that could comfort him and he wanted Ben to sit next to him and hold his hand. Whenever Ben got tired of that, Ricky went back to being cantankerous. When they got out of the car he clung to Rachel and wanted nothing to do with TJ.

"What's this all about?" TJ whispered to Rachel at one of the many stops along the way.

"I really don't know." Rachel shrugged her shoulders. His behavior was as much a surprise to her as anyone. "Maybe it just feels too unsettled for him."

"And unsettled enough for Ben to feel comfortable?" TJ asked. Rachel could see the weariness in his eyes.

"Well, maybe on a trip Ben doesn't have to work so hard to convince us he doesn't want to stay." She chuckled. "Maybe it's his vacation."

"And ours, if Ricky would just mellow out," TJ sighed.

The Metcafes caravanned with them, bringing their truck to help haul the college girls' furniture and belongings home.

16

Mary traveled in the truck with Annie, the Metcafe's youngest daughter. They offered to have Ben ride with them for a while. He eagerly agreed despite Ricky's cries and traveled the remainder of the trip with Mike and Tina. Rachel moved to the backseat to be with Ricky. He calmed down enough or wore himself out enough to sleep the last half hour of the trip.

It was the first time Tina and Mike had met the boys. Throughout the spring Tina had been on tour and of course both families had been busy with end-of-school activities.

"They really are adorable, Rache," Tina said as they were sitting in a restaurant where they had stopped for lunch. Tina watched TJ take the boys to the men's room to wash up. He was giving Ricky a piggyback ride, pretending to be his horse. It was the only way he could get Ricky to leave Rachel's side.

"I know. They steal your heart right off the bat, especially when I see them with TJ like that." She sighed. "It's been exhausting though. I'm so wiped out I sleep good at night—except for when Ben has bad dreams. Were we this tired when our girls were babies?"

"I know I was. I remember it felt like years before I slept through the night. But we were younger then, too, you know."

"Don't remind me." Rachel laughed. "It's a lot different parenting little kids in your twenties than when you're pushing fifty. It's a good thing I have all the camps but one directed by others this year. And that one I am directing is in July and it's co-directed. I can't get much done besides caring for the boys and neither can TJ. We keep hoping it will be better now that he isn't driving into Nashville every day for Ben's school."

The boys came back to the table. Ricky was uncharacteristically shy but Ben was the picture of a perfectly happy, well-adjusted little boy.

"Aunt Tina?" he asked using the name he heard the other

kids use.

Tina turned her attention to Ben.

"Mama says you sing on the radio."

Tina told him that was true and answered his questions about radio and music.

Rachel was stunned Ben had referred to her as his mother. As she tried to blink back tears at the profoundness of the simple moment, Tina went on to tell him what a big star TJ was. Rachel looked over at her husband to see if he had noticed but he and Mike were deep in conversation about baseball players. Oh, well, it wasn't like Ben had actually called her Mama. But it was the closest he had come to acknowledging her as such.

"Your Daddy and I have sung together a few times," Tina was saying. "Ben, have you ever been to a concert before?"

He shook his head.

"Well, you'll get your chance I'm sure."

Ben looked admiringly at her. The look on his face was that of a love-sick puppy and Rachel had to hold back a grin. Later she would tease Tina about Ben being in love.

Ricky leaned against Rachel, his thumb in his mouth, looking like he might fall asleep. Tina tried to engage him in the conversation but he just hid his face and wouldn't talk. Rachel was concerned about what had happened to their outgoing, energetic little boy. She looked over at TJ. He had stopped talking and was watching Ricky, too. He raised his eyebrows questioningly at Rachel but she just shrugged. She made a mental note to ask Lori about it when they got home.

The Ole' Miss graduation was held indoors and it was long for everyone, especially for the boys. They made it through the first part, fidgeting through speeches and music. They enjoyed clapping and cheering at first but soon got bored of hearing name after name. Thankfully, Beth and Laney were in the middle group so once they had received their diplomas Rachel and Tina were able to take the boys out and walk around the center. It was pleasant outside. The boys ran and played on the grassy hill by the auditorium. It was good to see Ricky acting more normally. Rachel had worried he was coming down with something.

The women sat on a bench and watched the boys while they talked about the girls, the upcoming graduation party and Beth and Laney's future plans. Laney had been offered a teaching job at the school the Metcafe and Keyton kids had attended since elementary school. Because it was a private school the pay was lower but Laney was excited to go home as a teacher. Beth, who was going to teach while working on her Master's in school counseling, had taken a job in a public school in Nashville. Though they would be in different school districts, Laney and Beth were looking into getting a place together. Beth would be teaching third grade while Laney would be teaching first. Rachel wondered if the boys attended Heritage Elementary if Laney would be Ben's teacher.

"It'll be nice to have the girls closer to home," Tina commented.

Rachel agreed. Beth had been double majoring in child development and education. She had taken some courses during the summer so her visits home had been short and infrequent.

"How are the others holding up with the new kids on the block?" Tina asked, pointing toward the boys.

"They have been pretty busy with school, work and of course, softball this spring, so it hasn't been as dramatic for them as it has been for us," Rachel answered honestly. "Naomi has been great with the boys, especially Ben, who, by the way, has done a complete one-eighty on this trip. What you see is not the same Ben we have had at home the last couple of weeks. But I like this Ben and hope to see more of him."

Tina laughed. "TJ told Mike it's like the rest of the world stopped and overnight everything became about these boys."

Rachel nodded. "He's been at the school with Ben almost every day. I went in a few times so he could get work done at home or for Hope E. and catch up on his other business stuff. I even took Ricky with me the last day of school since he hates it when I'm gone. Naomi has helped out a couple of times with Ben when I had clients or training or if TJ was busy. Mary, Gracie and Emily all do fine with Ricky, too. Next fall we will have them in school closer to home. But from what I am hearing from our adoption support group we will be at the school a great deal this first year. When your kids get older you forget how much you have to do for little ones. It's been non-stop."

"I don't know how you do it," Tina said. "I don't know if I could start over and do all that again. Annie will graduate in a few years. I will finally able to start really touring again. But mostly, I don't think I would have the energy. Look at those boys!"

Rachel and Tina laughed watching Ben and Ricky running and chasing each other through the trees.

"Well," Rachel sighed, "I am not chasing them around the way I chased the girls when I was younger, that's for sure! But I'll tell you, Tina, I am so thankful for TJ. It is amazing having someone to lean on. I parented so long by myself maybe that makes me appreciate him more."

The boys came over for a quick drink from their juice boxes and then ran off again. Rachel leaned closer to Tina and whispered, "I seriously don't think there is anything sexier than a man being a dad to his kids."

"You said it, sister!" Tina agreed. "The way Mike treated

Laney when we first met stole my heart. Too bad more men don't understand that."

"Speaking of dads, we better get back before the final part of the graduation," Rachel said. She called the boys over. Despite their protests at having to go back into the building, they headed toward the auditorium. If Ben hadn't been so set on impressing his Aunt Tina, Rachel was sure he would have had one of his transition tantrums. Rachel had been expecting it. But instead, he turned on the charm and ran ahead of Rachel and Ricky to Tina and asked shyly if he could hold her hand.

"Sure, darlin'." Tina took his hand.

Ben looked over his shoulder at Rachel with a devious smile that said, "Watch this." Then he looked up at Tina with an open expression of love and adoration. "Too bad you're not my new mama."

Rachel took in deep breath. You could have all the knowledge in the world but a punch was still a punch. When Ben cunningly looked back at her to see her reaction she pretended she had not heard or seen anything. But after he turned back toward Tina, Rachel pressed her hand to her chest where it felt like the blow had landed. "Like you, Jesus," she prayed. "Help me love these boys like you do."

chapter

"Do you have any ideas about why Ricky had such a hard time on our last trip?"

Rachel placed a cup of coffee on the table in front of Lori who had come to the farm for a home visit. TJ had taken the boys with him to the barn for some chores so Lori and Rachel could talk.

"Ricky?" Lori looked puzzled. "I thought he was doing well."

Rachel filled her in on the past weekend.

"Maybe he was worried you were taking him to another place to live."

"I don't know, Lori. He was really upset. Do you think he would tell you what was bothering him? I am trying to move out of the therapist role here. But he was too freaked out to talk to me about it anyway. Ben might even know what was going on. He trusts you. Maybe he would fill you in."

Lori said she would try talking to him. "By the way, Rachel, are you going to contact a new therapist for the boys?"

"I want to. I was thinking a family therapist might be good for all of us. I know where I would go if we were in Colorado. I still consult with my mentor back home. But what about around here?"

"When you can't see my families, I usually recommend Dr. Anderson," Lori said.

Rachel had recently attended a workshop he put on for therapists working with abused kids. She didn't know he was seeing clients.

Lori added, "I will see what we can do. If you can get in he would be great."

Rachel agreed. She had used his materials for both camp training and her personal work with children and families. His work was in agreement with other experts in the field Rachel held in high esteem such as Dr. Bruce Perry and Dr. Dave

Ziegler, giants in the field of childhood trauma.

"Speaking of Dr. Anderson," Rachel added, "You know he would say we should put a team together as a support system. Maybe things will be better after the summer but last year Ben sure could have used a team working with the school."

"I know." Lori shook her head. "We should start getting that set up before school starts. We should start talking to the school as soon as possible."

Rachel and TJ had been talking about this already. It had been recommended that the team be any and all willing people in the children's lives so everyone could offer support. Ben was slightly delayed in reading and he had an IEP due to his social issues and behavioral problems. For Rachel the IEP was a passport to get services and extra support for Ben at school. Parents had the right to decide who was on a child's IEP team. Rachel had helped other parents advocate for their kids. Some schools were better at working with IEPs than others just as some teams were better at working with parents to bridge the gap between school and home.

Everything Rachel believed about helping kids with attachment issues and overcoming their trauma was wrapped up in a collaborative effort between all the caring adults in the child's life. She had been in the therapist role on support teams but this would be her first experience working with the school system in the parent role.

"Well, I'd better go meet with the boys," Lori said putting her coffee cup on the table near the sofa. "Can I talk with you and TJ when we are done?" Lori stood. "Should I go out to the barn?"

"Depends on what kind of visit you want," Rachel offered. "Out there Ricky will yak your ear off about the horses. I can call them up to the house and you can talk by the pool or go for a walk."

"I don't mind going down and getting them. We can walk and talk." Lori had been out to the farm several times to participate in the equine therapy with other children in her caseload.

"I'll walk down with you and maybe catch a moment with my husband while you have the boys," Rachel volunteered.

At the barn, the kids were playing in a fort TJ and Buck had made with the hay. When they saw Lori, Ricky came out and gave her a hug but as usual, Ben pulled back. He wanted to keep playing. Lori said she could talk to them in the fort or they could go for a walk and show her the old barn. That was met with enthusiasm since TJ never allowed them to play down there alone. They were eager to see the mysteries it held even if it meant talking with Lori.

Rachel and TJ walked back up to the house while Lori and boys headed down the driveway. By the time Lori had talked to Ben and Ricky together and then separately, Rachel had prepared lunch and made a few phone calls to set up the final training for camp counselors later that month.

TJ had gone to his office, also taking care of phone calls. Typically spring and summer were crazy busy, getting the summer programs organized. Thankfully they had a great staff and core of volunteers because even with TJ's boundless energy there was no way they could get everything ready by themselves.

By the time Lori and the boys entered the house it was warm outside and they all looked sweaty and dirty. Rachel sent the boys to the bathroom to clean up for lunch. She got them settled at the table to eat with instructions to go to their rooms afterward and play so the adults could talk. TJ, Rachel and Lori went into the family room for a short visit.

"Well, you two might be having a difficult time," she

began, "maybe one of the most challenging years of your life. But let me say first off, you all are doing a great job." Lori smiled encouragingly. "Ricky is, of course, enthusiastic about staying and quick to say how much he loves everything from the animals to his new sisters. Ben talks about swimming and fishing with his dad." She pointed to TJ. "He referred to you several times as 'Dad.' But—" She looked compassionately at Rachel. "—he wouldn't say much about staying or wanting to stay. When I asked him how it was going with you, Rachel, he said, 'Okay, I guess.' Even though he is fighting to remain indifferent he told me all about the trip to Mississippi and about the fun stuff he was going to get to do this summer. He talks about this place as home. So don't lose heart."

TJ asked Lori about Ricky's behavior on the trip. "He was so freaked out. Did you tell her about it, Rache?"

"Yes," Lori said. "Rachel and I talked about it and so did Ricky and I. I asked him how it went and he said he liked it here best. When I pressed him a bit more about traveling he just said he thought he might get left behind. His vocabulary is more limited than Ben's so it's tough to know what he is thinking. But he did tell me that trips scare him."

"Did Ben tell you anything that might give us a clue?" Rachel asked. "We know their mother abandoned them more than once. Maybe she left Ricky in a new place or with other people."

"Ben didn't offer much. He's got stuff locked in there pretty deep. Talking about what happened with his mom has never been easy for Ben. He did tell me Ricky was scared they would go away on a trip and be left. I asked him if that happened before. He shrugged his shoulders like it was no big deal and casually said that one time she left them at a gas station. He was quick to defend her by saying she came back later."

TJ swore under his breath. Rachel was silent, stunned.

Poor babies. Rachel thought about the fear they both must have felt.

"Ricky was just a baby, Ben told me. I can double check the reports and see if I find anything on the incident," Lori offered. "Sounds like he was too young to remember what actually happened."

"Well," Rachel said, "our bodies remember things our minds may not consciously be aware of. The feelings of being abandoned and the fear of it happening again could still have triggered even if he had no memory of it."

"Can you imagine the fear Ricky must have been experiencing at every stop?" TJ commented.

"No wonder," Rachel said thinking back about the boys' changes in behavior. "And Ben, sure that this time we were leaving him, tried to be so good we wouldn't drop them off. Wow." Rachel looked at Lori and shook her head. "Can you check and see if that happened more than once? It would be good to know as much as possible about the boys and what happened. At least next time we go somewhere we will know what is going on."

Rachel glanced at TJ. He agreed.

"Maybe we'll have to fly next time just to change it all up. They were probably never left at an airport." He shook his head in disbelief. "Damn."

"On a lighter note," Lori said, "Ben told me all about how you were a big country music star and how Aunt Tina played your songs for him in her truck. He was pretty enthusiastic about learning to sing and play guitar so he could go on stage with Tina."

TJ laughed. "Well, we noticed he was a little taken with her."

"Other than that, everything is on target for how they are doing. Do you need anything else from me?"

Rachel and TJ glanced at one another. Rachel saw the weariness in his eyes and wondered if hers were the same. She told Lori she would check into Dr. Anderson and reminded Lori that Ben would be at camp in a couple of weeks.

"Make sure you both get some time for yourselves," Lori reminded them, saying good-bye at the door.

Rachel was surprised how foreign that sounded already and the boys had only been there a month. She looked up at TJ. "'Time for ourselves?' Have you noticed any of that in the last few weeks?"

"Not really." He gave a mirthless laugh and led her to the family room. The boys were in their rooms, quiet. Rachel thought about checking on them, but she could tell TJ needed her attention at the moment.

"Rache, now that school is out, can we set a schedule for the summer? I gotta have time to get some work done around here and for Hope E. I know you have clients and we've got camps coming up. What do you think?"

She sat close to him and reached for his hand. "I think it would help all of us. And I was wondering, TJ, if maybe we should hire some extra help with the stuff that doesn't need our personal attention."

"Already ahead of you, Babe. I talked to Tucker about working with Buck, taking care of the farm chores I usually help with. I enjoy working the farm but right now when I am here I need to make sure I have enough time with the kids. Besides, Tucker wanted to work more this summer and you and I both know Tucker wants to be close by." He patted her hand. "What about you? Do you have enough help with the housework or should we see if Susan can come an extra day? What about childcare for the summer when you have clients and what not?"

"The house has been fine with the help three days. Sometimes I wish we had a cook but the girls have been pitching in." Rachel laughed thinking about how much the boys could eat. "As far as childcare, Naomi's work schedule is set so we just have to coordinate with her for when she is available to help me here. The three of us can also tag team it with the boys to work around clients. And the younger girls offered to help for short periods. The other kids are running the riding program this summer." Rachel broke off, thinking about how great it was having their kids working the programs she had built.

"I really don't want to leave Ben too much yet," Rachel said as she thought about his attachment issues. "He seems to bond with others just to prove he doesn't need us—well, me. Did you see him with Tina over the weekend?"

TJ nodded. He gave her a hug and encouraged her, "He's crazy about you, Babe. He just can't let himself be loved yet." Shaking his head as he mentioned their abuse, he said, "Boy, that was something, what Lori told us about them being left like that. Wonder what other crap has happened to them. Makes a lot of sense how freaked out Ricky was."

Rachel nodded. "There is always a reason for every behavior. Speaking of which, the boys are awfully quiet. I'd better go check it out."

"Okay. I'll get that summer schedule thing done and you can look it over. We can always adjust it. I know with school out you'll probably be here at the farm a lot with the kids." He got up to give her a hug and to head downstairs to work. "You want me to check on the boys?"

"No, I've got it." She kissed him and went down the hall. Things did seem way too quiet. She opened Ricky's door but he wasn't in his room. Rachel felt her heart miss a beat. She waited outside Ben's door and prayed that whatever she found there she would be calm. She opened it slowly. She half expected the room to be in shambles but it wasn't. Actually, there wasn't much left there to wreck. There were a few toys and the normal heap of clothes on the floor. A few things stuck out of dresser drawers. Otherwise, things appeared undisturbed.

Her eyes were drawn to the bed. It was piled with stuffed animals that must have come from Ricky's room since Ben had destroyed nearly all of his. Then through the toys she spotted the boys, both sound asleep. Tucked in with his favorite horses, Ricky's thumb disappeared into his mouth. His free hand hung over the side of the bed where Ben lay on the floor with the top blanket from his bed. He had fallen asleep holding Ricky's hand.

She stood absolutely still, watching them. It hit her sometimes at moments like these how much they meant to each other. She thought about Ricky scared on the trip and Ben holding his hand, how close together they stood when she first met them and Ricky coming to get her when Ben had bad dreams. No matter how difficult it got with Ben she knew keeping the boys together was as important as helping them find their individuality and autonomy.

chapter

The Little Girl

All of her earliest memories had her brother John in them. She could picture him perfectly and place his face in every past experience until she was six. But except for the screaming and terrible words shouted at her, Rachel could hardly remember anything about her birth mother.

When Rachel brought to mind her old house and her old life, she felt empty. She felt she had been unwanted and unloved. In those dark memories echoed the words, "I hate you! You are ruining my life! I wish you had never been born." They haunted her and they motivated her. She would show them, she thought. She would prove she was worthy of love or at least worthy to be alive!

Her new family didn't say such things. They didn't hit and they didn't yell. But they never said they really wanted her either. She worried about that a lot. Would anyone ever be glad she was around? Once, during the first year at the Lewis house, her new mom asked if she wouldn't like to go live with another family.

Having to leave and move again terrified her. Rachel thought it was a sure sign they were looking for a reason to send her away. They had sent John away and she didn't even know why. Of course, he was always getting into trouble, and he usually dragged her into it as well, which meant they were both in trouble all the time. So why did they send John away and not her? Maybe they were still looking for another place to send her. If they thought he was bad they surely thought the same thing about her.

Remembering John made her miss him. She didn't miss him blaming her and saddling her with guilt for the problems he created or the way he bullied her into doing whatever he wanted. Life was easier without him in some ways, for sure.

But not having her big brother meant she had no one. Without John she felt lost and abandoned. John was the one person she had to go through life with, the only one that really understood the hard times they had been through. She wondered if she would ever see him again.

At least she had God. As long as she could remember she had always been able to talk to God and knew He was with her. He was the one constant in her life from long before she could remember.

Even though she missed John and wasn't sure this family loved her she didn't want to be sent away. She didn't want to go back to the Wilcox house, to smelly old Mr. Wilcox and his nightly visits or to screaming Mrs. Wilcox who didn't have an affectionate bone in her body. She didn't want to get sent to another place where people yelled or hit or worse. She missed her grandmother and feeling like she belonged, but she didn't miss the anxiety of not getting enough to eat or fearing what was coming next. No, she didn't want to go to another family or back to her old family. She just wanted to know where she fit in and that she belonged to someone.

That is why she had to make it work here. If she tried harder maybe she could make her new parents proud that she was their kid. She was sure she could do it, earn their approval. She would be quiet and good. She would do what they told her and never talk back. John was always talking back and they sent him away. Maybe that was why.

Rachel made up her mind. She wouldn't tell them about all the bad stuff with Mr. Wilcox or how much trouble she had been in with John. She would try—try hard—to fit in. And maybe, just maybe, if she acted normal and didn't talk about being adopted, or worse, being a foster kid, she would be normal and everyone would treat her like she actually was the only thing she really wanted to be, someone's real daughter.

chapter

It was mid-summer, hot and humid. For Rachel and the kids mornings were filled with horses, long afternoons with swimming and evenings with baseball. And every day brought lots of sunshine.

While the older kids were in and out of the house all summer between jobs and friends, Rachel and boys spent most afternoons by the pool. Mary was home more than her sisters so many days she and her friends joined them. When TJ got off work early he would take Ricky and Ben and whoever was willing out to the pond. The boys would fish, skip rocks or build forts in the trees. Naomi split her time between work and helping Rachel with equine therapy or with the boys. Though life was busy, their days settled into a regular schedule and the boys seemed to be adjusting.

Their new routine included horseback riding lessons, chores, swimming lessons and time for exploring and playing on the farm. A lot of evenings after dinner, when it started to cool down, the older kids brought their various friends or boyfriends over. Almost weekly there was a group having a bonfire and music jam or other social event.

Usually the boys were in bed early but sometimes they would be allowed to stay up later. When that happened they would run around catching fireflies or roasting marshmallows with the other kids. A few times they joined the Metcafes to play softball. Laney and Beth were always easy to persuade to come to the family games.

At those times Rachel felt especially thankful for their big family and close friends. She had always been grateful for their family and their friendship with the Metcafes but watching how everyone embraced Ben and Ricky made Rachel realize afresh how valuable the sense of community and belonging was to them all. Everyone was so good about including the boys in the circle.

In July, Ben went to camp. Although the previous year he had been part of the day camp for younger kids, this was his first overnight camp. Rachel was co-directing as a new director was in training to take over.

There were similar camps taking place all over the nation designed for children ages seven through eleven in foster care that had been abused. Rachel had started the camp in for Franklin County, and directed several of the camps in the past both in Colorado and one in Nashville. But this year, since the new director was completely managing the camp, she was able to take a back seat and enjoy the kids. That made it possible for Ricky to come up for a couple of days.

TJ dropped Ricky off when he came to bring supplies and to be part of the big annual birthday party and Have-a-Go Show, a talent show the children put on. Since the boys' adoption process would likely be completed before next summer this was the only time they would be coming to this particular camp. The older girl campers loved Ricky and the staff enjoyed having him around as well. Whenever Rachel was needed somewhere there was always someone willing to watch out for Ricky.

That camp was, for Ben, the best and the worse week of his life. His counselor buddy, Matt, was one of Rachel's most experienced volunteers, but even so, she could tell Ben was putting him to the test. Matt had his hands full. Ben, typical of many of the boys, was quick to fight, non-cooperative and refused to allow Matt to get close to him. When they were alone together there were times Ben seemed to be having fun. He enjoyed the activities—swimming in the lake, paddling the canoes, and making wood projects. Mostly, he liked being in charge of what they did. But other times he was aggressive with the other boys and toward Matt. He could not be around other campers without instigating a fight. Matt was excellent at redirecting Ben's negative energies but Rachel could tell Ben was stretching him to his limit.

Chapel times, the birthday party, meals and game times were not going well. At camp, rather than punish kids, the goal was to move in closer and offer support. By Tuesday extra staff members were needed to help Matt keep Ben safe and to keep other kids safe around him. They did their best to surrounding him with encouragement and support. Ben was also having bad dreams.

Thursday night all the kids got awards. The eleven-year-olds went through a graduation of sorts. It was often the most challenging day. The campers were sad that camp was ending and they would soon be going home.

Rachel knew Ben and Matt struggled that day. As they headed into the building for the evening program she could tell Ben was not going to make it through without a blow up. Twice they had to move him away from another boy he was intent on fighting with. The boys had been at each other all week even though they had been moved into different rooms and the counselors tried to keep them apart. It always amazed Rachel how two kids with the same problems continually found each other despite saying they hated each other. When Matt tried to move Ben to different seat, Ben came unglued. Taking a swing at Matt, he bellowed, "I hate your guts! This stupid camp sucks!" He ran out of the chapel, dodging adults trying to grab him.

Rachel stood near one doorway with the camp director at the other. Matt was right behind Ben who had chosen to go through Rachel's door. She didn't try to grab him. She doubted he even noticed her as he pushed his way through.

Instead, she advised Matt to let him go but to stay as close as
he could. Rachel let the director know she would go out with
Matt and Ben in order to uphold the two-deep policy. It
mandated that at least two adults be with a child when away
from the group.

Ben had run down the hill. He had found a stick and
struck the trees with it as he circled the meadow area, swearing
and agitated. Rachel watched Matt move in as close as he
could. Ben was having none of it.

"Go away! I hate you!" Ben shouted.

"I can't leave you, Bud," Matt called out calmly. "But you
don't have to go back in there. We can stay out here."

"No! I want you to go away! Leave me alone!"

"I'll just stay this far away and follow you so you are safe,
okay?" Matt was using all his camp training, allowing the child
to lead and reassuring the child he was there only to protect.

Ben swore again. "Go away! Don't you get it? I hate you! I
hate this camp!" Rachel prayed as she watched Ben shout and
swing his stick, mad at the world and so afraid of caring about
anyone. Matt was perfect, talking calmly, staying out of range
but letting Ben know he was there for him. A couple of times
he tried to move in but Ben wasn't allowing him to get too
close. More than once he picked up a pine cone and threw it
at Matt's head. Matt ducked easily enough and continued to
reassure him.

They walked around and around. It took a long time but
Rachel noticed the circles getting smaller. Ben was still kicking
the dirt, muttering obscenities and occasionally throwing
things but he was allowing Matt to come closer. Rachel kept
praying and Matt kept talking to him calmly. She couldn't hear
what he was saying but she could see Ben wearing down.

A staff member came to Rachel to ask where the Bibles

were for the graduation. She turned her attention from Matt and Ben for a moment. By the time she had answered the question, Matt and Ben were standing very close together. Ben had the stick in his hand at his side and Matt was talking softly to him. Then as if by magical force, Ben dropped the stick and went down to his knees. He was crying. Matt knelt and wrapped his arms around him. They sat there together in the field while Ben cried and cried. His sounds were muffled but his body shook with sobs. Rachel realized she had never seen Ben cry this way even when he got hurt. This was the first real breaking point she had seen.

Matt motioned for her to come. Rachel was hesitant, not wanting to intrude on what was happening with the two of them but Matt insisted. As she came down the hill she prayed for wisdom. When she got closer she could hear Ben and she realized why Matt had called for her. She knelt beside Ben and put her hand on his arm. He looked up at her, his eyes filled with tears and his nose running. For the first time, he moved toward her and crawled into her lap. "I'm sorry, Mama," he cried over and over as he clung to her neck.

Rachel choked back sobs. "It's okay, precious boy. I love you. We love you." She pulled Matt in, too. "Benny, we love you." She whispered the words into his soft brown hair. "It's alright, son. You don't have to fight so hard. We'll protect you, baby."

Matt, Rachel and Ben huddled in the middle of the game field and held onto each other as God did what only He could do. He softened a boy's heart that had no weapon against unconditional love, safety and peace.

Later, Rachel would look back to that moment as marking a real change for Ben. He always called her Mama after that, a simple thing that meant a lot to her. He continued to struggle with his temper but he no longer fought against being with the family. He had, in his own way, come home.

That day at camp had been a life-changing experience for Matt, too. He told Rachel later that he had never seen the power of Jesus' acceptance, grace and love played out like that before. Matt said the whole time Ben was yelling and pacing down on the field, he just felt this overwhelming calm and love pouring through him onto that hurt little guy. Even while he was fighting off pine cones, all Matt could do was love and offer a safe place.

"It was incredible. I never felt so much a part of Jesus' heart," Matt said. Rachel asked him why Ben had called for her. Matt looked at her incredulously. "He was always asking for you. Didn't you know?"

"What do you mean? He never even called me Mama before that."

"I had no idea." Matt shook his head. "Every night when he had nightmares he woke up crying for you. When he finally let go down on the field, he was sobbing, 'Get my mama. I want my Mama.'"

Rachel cried when Matt told her. She couldn't help it. She hugged Matt and thanked him for loving Ben all week. After that incident she went into her little cabin, knelt by the bed and thanked God. Then she had called TJ and they both cried and rejoiced.

When people asked Rachel how camp, just one week, could make such a difference, Rachel had lots of stories of kids like Ben and counselors like Matt. Over the years she had collected hundreds of such examples. That was what kept her going year after year. But when the story was about your kid and how your own life was changed, well, there were no words for what Rachel felt about that one little week of camp.

chapter

The Little Boy

"Hey, Son, you can't keep fighting everyone forever."

Grandpa Eddie put his hand on Troy's broad shoulder. Troy loved his grandpa. Never having a dad, a real dad, Grandpa was the man who would talk to him and do stuff with him. Like now. Grandpa had heard about the latest fight and asked Troy to go for a walk. It was just the sort of thing he imagined his dad would do with him someday, if he ever came back.

Troy nodded as if he understood what Grandpa meant about not fighting everyone. He touched his swollen cheek under his blackened eye. It wasn't like he planned on getting into these fights.

"Grandpa?" Troy hesitated. He wanted to tell him about the fight, why he had to fight, but he didn't want Grandpa to think less of him. He wondered if telling Grandpa would help.

When Troy was ten, Grandpa Eddie had married Troy's grandmother. That was two years ago and right around the time Troy, Julie and their mom moved down the street. At first, Troy doubted Eddie. His distrust of men ran deep. He figured it was just a matter of time before Eddie moved on or turned mean. But he didn't. He was patient and he took an interest in Troy. He told Troy he had always wanted a grandson. Secretly, Troy had always wanted a dad but he didn't tell anyone that. After a while, Troy came to realize that having a Grandpa was pretty good.

Grandpa was the one that got him into Little League and Pop Warner football and took the time to play catch and told Troy things that helped him play better. He went to all Troy's games and even occasionally took him to big league games. Every Monday night during football season Grandpa and Grandma had Troy and Julie come over for Monday night football. Last week, their mom had the night off and came, too. For the first time it felt like a family. Like how Troy thought a family should be.

Grandpa Eddie helped their mom a lot but the thing that really won Troy over was how good he treated Grandma. Grandma had always been there for Troy and Julie and their mom. Grandpa Eddie was the first man Troy knew that demonstrated how a guy should treat a woman.

Watching football on Monday nights or going places with them, Troy was like a sponge soaking up their teasing and playfulness. He liked the way Grandpa Eddie spoke to Grandma and about her. Troy didn't know much about girls but he figured when he had a girlfriend, Grandpa Eddie would teach him what to do.

"Grandpa?" He started again. "Can I tell you something?"

"Sure, Son. Speak your mind."

"I don't want to keep fighting. It just—happens. And once I start, well, I get so mad— The thing is, when I get mad like that I don't think I can stop it. I feel it when I play football sometimes, too, like a monster inside me. I don't like it. I try to stop it but I don't think I can. Do you ever feel like that?"

Grandpa Eddie told him he used to fight a lot when he was younger. "Troy let me ask you, what do you think you are so mad about?"

"Well, it's just the stupid jerks—"

"No, Son, what are you really mad about?" Grandpa stopped walking and faced him.

Troy shook his head, biting his lower lip. He looked down at his hand, bruised from yesterday's fight. He thought about the stuff kids said that usually earned the first punch. "I don't know, Grandpa. Deep in here—" Troy put his hand on his chest. "—it feels so wild, like a storm. It feels bad in here." He tapped his chest.

Grandpa Eddie nodded. "In that storm the wind is blowing. Think for a moment. Can you hear the wind? I think it is saying something to you but you have to listen hard to hear it."

Troy shook his head but Grandpa encouraged him to just listen. Biting his lip, his eyes threatened to fill with tears as he thought about the storm inside him. Then he replied softly, "I just feel rotten and angry all the time even when things are good." He looked into his grandpa's eyes to see if he understood.

Grandpa nodded. "Listen, Son," he insisted. "You have to listen to that storm in you and find out what it is saying."

Troy shook his head.

"Anger is just a cover that pushes people away. Do you have a secret in there, Son?"

Swallowing hard, Troy thought about his mother and Julie being pushed around by George and how scared he was hiding in the closest. At first, Troy felt the familiar anger start to wash over him. But then as he waited he could feel fear banging around in his chest. He fought to keep it pushed down. Fear made him feel small and helpless. When he let the anger out he felt strong. He could hear George's voice. "You're so worthless I can't even waste my time hitting you."

Tears stung his eyes. He looked up at his Grandpa. He knew what the wind was saying in the dark of his soul. It told him he was nothing, that he would never be anything or do anything right. In a choked voice, Troy said softly, "I'm no good." He tried not to cry. He never cried in front of anybody but the tears fell on their own accord. "Maybe I will never amount to anything."

Grandpa Eddie pulled Troy into a hug and held him tight. "Troy you are good at everything you do—sports, school and certainly at winning fights." He gave a short chuckle. "You can spend your whole life trying to prove yourself. But maybe you don't know how much you matter."

Troy shook his head.

Grandpa continued, "Do you know how much you are worth, Troy—to me, to your mama, to God? Do you know how much your mama loves you? How much Grandma and I love and care you for? We pray for you all the time. Do you know how much you mean to your little sister? She worships the ground you walk on. Son, you are a good boy and we love you." While Grandpa was telling him all these things Troy tried to let them sink in but he kept shaking his head. It was hard to believe the good stuff. For some reason, the bad stuff seemed louder in his head.

Besides, he thought if he mattered to his mom why didn't she get rid of George before George beat the crap out of him and went after Julie? How could his sister ever forgive him for letting her get hurt when he had promised to protect her? If he really mattered, why did his real dad leave and never even try to find him? And he might be good at all those things Grandpa said, but that was easy stuff. Troy didn't feel good inside. He felt just like George had said, worthless. And around the worthlessness was this fear that everyone would find out what he really was.

He shook his head again. What if Grandpa knew all the hate in him and the weakness and how scared he was that inside he was as bad as George? Why else did he fight so much and hit so hard?

He stood there, shifting his feet, feeling uncomfortable. He wondered how much he could really tell Grandpa Eddie and risk betraying his mother and himself.

Grandpa Eddie seemed to sense his indecision. "You want

to tell me about it?" He pointed to a group of trees and invited Troy to come sit with him. "Come on, Son."

Troy stood there a moment searching his grandpa's face then shrugged his shoulders and followed him to the spot. Grandpa Eddie sat down on an old log but Troy stood. He kicked at the dirt a little and said he wasn't sure what to say. Finally he started talking about his dad leaving him and then about his mom and George. As he opened up, tears flowed. At times he shouted as the anger and helplessness poured out of him. He told Grandpa everything. He even told him about the nightmares and his fears and finally his hurt and pain.

"I hate him!" Troy shouted.

"Hate, who?"

"George! No, you know what? I hate my dad for leaving us. It's his fault. If he hadn't left George would never have come. Why did he leave us? Didn't he think we might need him?"

Through all of it, Grandpa just listened, letting him vent and yell. Finally, totally spent, Troy sat down, buried his head in his arms and sobbed. Grandpa put his hand on his back and let him cry.

"I don't understand it," Troy said weakly.

"No one could," Grandpa agreed. And he held him close. "You are a brave kid though. I am glad you shared all that with me. That's really tough."

They sat quietly for a while. His head hurt from crying and all the emotion of it but he felt like a ton of bricks had been taken from his shoulders. He looked at Grandpa Eddie who seemed to be thinking deeply. He just fiddled with his ring, not saying anything.

"What, Grandpa?"

"Well, I was just thinking how much you have been carrying around. And I was thinking you must trust me a lot to say all that."

Troy nodded.

"I am real proud of you, boy. But I can't make all this better for you. Now listen carefully. Troy, I love you and telling me was good. But God loves you even more than I do and only He can really take this stuff from you. Do you want to let Him get rid of it for you? Do you understand?"

Troy nodded slowly. "You mean I need to tell it to God."

"Yes. Ask Him what to do about it when you're done. Troy, do you remember when you asked Jesus into your heart?"

Troy nodded again. He and his mom had both gone forward one Sunday a few months ago and asked Jesus into their lives. "Well, Son, He lives in you and He already has the answer to all this but he wants you to trust Him like you did me and tell him about it."

"Can we do it together? I mean, right now?"

"Sure enough. You just go ahead and I will be right here with you. Think about Him being here with the two of us and you just say what you need to say."

Troy closed his eyes and thought about Jesus standing there in front of the old log. He imagined Jesus ready to listen and he could feel His love reaching out to him. "Okay."

Troy hadn't learned any fancy prayers. He just laid it on the line in the most simple and straightforward way he knew how. "Jesus. I have been really mad—at my dad, at George, at my mom and even at you—for all the bad stuff that has happened to me and my family. But now that I told Grandpa all about it, I don't feel so bad anymore. I am sorry for hating everyone and wanting to hurt people. I am sorry for—for making other people pay for what my dad and George did. I don't know if you can fix it, or fix me, but if you could just forgive me and take all this bad stuff away from me that would help a lot."

He imagined Jesus agreeing. Telling Grandpa had felt like it calmed the storm inside him, but telling Jesus was like taking all the bad memories, thoughts and feelings he had boxed up and handing it all to Jesus and Jesus taking the box and carrying it away.

When he was done, Grandpa Eddie prayed and thanked Jesus for taking care of Troy, his mama and Julie. He thanked Jesus for carrying this load for Troy and taking it away from him. They embraced and Grandpa told Troy again how proud of him he was.

Troy felt free. More free than he had ever felt before.

chapter

The day started out better than the best. For one thing, Rachel slept in, which was rare for her. It was only an hour later than she usually got up. It felt so good. Even when they had late nights she was normally up early so she could catch a bit of quiet time to herself before the day began. But this morning she was awakened by TJ coming over to sit on her side of the bed. He had been up for a while checking on the horses and getting things ready for Tucker and Buck. Since it was so warm they had been trying to get big projects done before the heat of the day.

"Hey. Babe," he said tenderly as she opened her eyes and felt his caress on her face. He smelled like sweet hay, summer and something else she could never quite name. She took in a deep breath as she came fully awake. "Got some coffee here for you." He held a mug of her favorite brew. She sat up and took a sip.

"Mmmm. Just right." She smiled at him. He leaned in and gave her a warm kiss. "Thanks," she breathed. "What is this for?" She was trying to remember if it was an anniversary or something she should have remembered. She was coming up blank. "Is it a special day?" He was great at surprises and even though it had been a while since she had seen it, he had an incredibly romantic side. The summer, graduations and adding to their family and parenting duties hadn't allowed much time or energy for their relationship. TJ smiled at her, his eyes bright and full of light and fun.

He shook his head and told her it just a Tuesday.

"Okay, then what?"

He tried to look offended, as if there had to be a reason for him bringing her coffee in bed. But his goofy grin gave him away. "Hon, it's been a while since—you know—and each night we both fall into bed completely exhausted. The boys will be asleep for a while longer. But I need you, Babe." He took the cup from her hand and eased himself into the bed with her.

"You need me?" she asked teasingly. "What makes your needs higher than everyone else's in this house that needs me?"

TJ put his hand on her waist and pulled her a little closer. "Cause you need me, too. What I do, I'm doing for both of us." He smiled and winked.

Rachel laughed. She reached up and pulled his face down to meet hers and their kisses increased as passion met both their needs.

"Thanks for waking me up," she told him later. She watched him putting on his clothes. "You were right. I did need you, even more than I needed sleep."

"My pleasure, ma'am," he grinned.

Rachel ran a hand through her hair. She felt so blessed and happy. Things had been going well with the boys and the other kids.

TJ came to where she was getting dressed and took her in his arms. She leaned her head against his chest while he held her. "Rachel?" She looked up to his face. "I love you."

"I love you, too." She replied.

He leaned down to kiss her lips, a kiss she returned readily, gratefully, somewhat hungrily.

TJ murmured his approval of her eagerness and Rachel thought they might end up lost in one another again.

The knock on the door startled them both. "Mama?" Ben's voice called out. Both TJ and Rachel jumped back guiltily even though the door was closed.

"Well," TJ said, "guess that's that."

Laughing, Rachel pecked his cheek. "For now."

Turning to open the door, a new joy welled in her at the sight of her oldest son. "Good morning, Ben."

He gave a quick greeting and let her know he was hungry. "Okay, let's go get you some breakfast."

That was the start of her day, a day she would not forget.

After breakfast she returned calls and worked on the list of things they needed to talk to the school about. Naomi had taken Ben and Ricky out to the pool. She had the day off. Later, after Tucker got off work, they planned to go do something together. Rachel figured she had about an hour to get her paperwork finished before the boys grew tired of swimming.

Looking at the Heritage Elementary School website, she was deep in thought. Although they planned for the boys attend the private school where all the other kids had gone, Rachel wasn't sure if it would have all the resources the boys might need. Could the staff handle the issues Ben and Ricky brought with them? She picked up the phone to make an appointment with the principal. The school was highly structured which would be good, but the students were required to meet high academic goals. Were the boys ready for that? Maybe by the time they were in junior or senior high—TJ's gentle knock on the office door interrupted her thoughts.

"Could you come with me a minute?" he asked.

What now? His face was serious though he wore a strained smile.

"Sure, Babe. What's up?" He just motioned for her to follow him to the living room. She was surprised to see Gracie and Danny sitting on the couch. Danny stood as she came in. Rachel said hello and glanced at Gracie. Her head was down and she fiddled with her hands the way TJ did when he was nervous.

The tension was thick in the little room. Rachel sat facing the kids and TJ pulled up a chair next to her. Danny sat again beside Gracie.

"What's going on?" Rachel couldn't see wasting any time with small talk. It was obvious something weighty needed to be said.

Danny cleared his throat. "Um—we, I, uh, Mrs. Keyton, we—"

Rachel felt her stomach sink. She looked to TJ but he, too, was focused on his hands.

Finally it was Gracie that looked up and said quickly, "Mom, I'm pregnant." She burst into tears and hung her head again. Danny reached over and held her hand. TJ shifted in his seat. Rachel could feel his tension.

"Did you know this already?" she asked him.

"Danny talked to me just now. I told him to go get Gracie while I went to get you."

Rachel let her breath out slowly, trying to take it all in. She turned to Danny and Gracie. "So, what are you going to do?" Her thoughts were racing. The reality of the situation was starting to hit her. Anger poured through her. Instead of being calm and asking the kinds of questions she might ask her clients, she blurted, "Geez, Danny, Gracie, we didn't even know you were dating!"

"That's exactly what I said," TJ added. "Gracie, how long have you known about this?"

Gracie looked up at her dad, tears glistening on her cheeks. "By the end of June I thought maybe— But I didn't take a test until after the Fourth of July party at the Metcafes. That's when I told Danny. We've been trying to figure out what to do."

Rachel's emotions were tossing between exasperation at feeling unexplainably betrayed and empathy for Gracie struggling with this on her own. TJ, on the other hand, obviously past the initial shock, was just plain mad.

"I cannot believe this. Or you." He pointed at Danny. "This is my daughter! How many conversations have we had over the years about sex and what I wanted for my girls? My God, Danny, how many times have we talked and all the while you were having sex—"

"Daddy!" Gracie jumped up indignantly. "It's not his fault. It wasn't like that. He wasn't being dishonest. We—we've loved each other for a long time and have been friends—but when it changed it just happened so fast. We—both wanted—"

"Hell, Grace Sue! I don't care what you wanted!" TJ started to stand then regained control. He sat on the edge of his seat, still speaking with a hard edge in his voice. "Maybe I don't have any call to be taking it out on him when it's really the both of you I am furious with."

He looked exasperated at both of them then pointing at Gracie said heatedly, "What would your mother say? Probably a good thing she didn't live to see this day."

TJ rubbed his hand on his jaw, a sure sign he was trying to calm down enough to think clearly. Rachel wanted to intervene but she knew TJ well enough to know he would want to speak his mind. Besides, she didn't know what to say. She had never heard him throw Kris and her memory at any of the kids like that before.

"I understand that you are upset, sir." Danny stood next to Gracie, putting his arm around her protectively.

"Young man, you don't know the half of it," TJ countered.

"I know, I know. I am sorry. I don't blame you for being mad. But we came to you because despite everything we know we need help. We need your help." He took Gracie's hand and tried to guide her to sit again but she shook her head at Danny and stubbornly stood her ground. She returned her father's glare.

"I don't know what Mama would say if she were here, Daddy, but she's not! I wish to God she were. Even though she would be mad at me, too, I still wish she were here to help me figure out what to do. I know we messed up and telling you was the worst thing I could imagine. We thought about just getting rid of it, not having to tell anyone, but in the end

I couldn't do that and neither could Danny. And I know Mama would at least be thankful about that."

Rachel was looking back and forth between TJ and Gracie. TJ didn't respond. He just motioned for them to sit. Rubbing his face boisterously, he took a deep breath and sighed.

"Look, you two, you guys have had a lot more time to think this through than we have. You need to give us some time to— um—what do you call it, Rachel, process? We need to have time to process this. Right now I don't know what to say. Honestly, it's all I can do to keep from hitting you, Danny, and there's no rationale to the thoughts running through my head." He looked at Rachel. "What do you think?"

She nodded in agreement. "You guys need to talk with us about this but we can't do that right now. I know telling us must have been really difficult and we don't want to make things worse by responding with our emotions. Speaking for me, I do need to just digest that you two are together, that you are obviously having sex and that you are carrying a baby, our grandchild."

Rachel was beginning to recover from her own shock and see what the kids were feeling. It was a lot to take in for sure. And saying it out loud stirred conflicting emotions in her.

TJ stood up and rubbed his hands on his jeans. Rachel came to stand next to him. "Give us today and tonight to sort this out in our minds. Then we can talk about it together. How about tomorrow morning about ten? Will that work for you, Rache? Can Naomi or Tina take the boys?"

Rachel nodded and said she would figure it out. Danny shook hands with TJ and he and Gracie started to leave together.

"Oh, no you don't." TJ stopped Gracie. "Right now, I can't deal with you being together. Danny, you go on home. Gracie, you are staying here," he said authoritatively. "Don't give me that look. You still live here and I still have a say about what you do."

Gracie started to protest but Danny put his hand on her arm. "No, Gracie, he's right. I'll go home. It's okay."

"Well, can I at least walk him out to his car and say good-bye?" she asked a little sarcastically.

"Three minutes and he is down the driveway," TJ said just as disdainfully.

Rachel almost laughed. She always thought Gracie was most like Kris of all the girls, but watching father and daughter butt heads and seeing TJ's pig-headedness in Gracie, she realized how alike they were.

TJ turned to walk away then stopped directly in front of Danny. "Don't push me, boy," he said somewhat threateningly.

"No sir," Danny responded quickly and militantly.

Gracie threw her hands in the air and rolled her eyes as she followed Danny outside.

TJ practically stomped to the master bedroom. Rachel followed. As she came into the room he turned and glared at her. "Rache," he said sharply, "I just need to be alone right now."

When she opened her mouth to respond he held up his hand to shut her off. "Please, I promise we'll talk, but let me blow off some steam for a while." He grabbed his hat and bolted past her.

Rachel exhaled. It wasn't like she didn't have anything to do and she knew he needed some space. But despite that, it was difficult for her when she couldn't talk things through with him. Talking about it was her way of processing. She sat on the bed and thought about Gracie, Danny and this new life coming into the world.

She didn't know what to do. There was really nothing she could say or do, let alone figure out what would happen next.

So she prayed. Rachel got down on her knees by the bed and prayed for the kids and then she prayed for TJ and for wisdom for both of them when they talked to Danny and Gracie. She prayed for their family and the other girls who would be finding out soon enough.

When she got up off her knees she felt better. She was more peaceful and able to deal with whatever they needed to do next. She went out to the pool to check on Naomi and the boys.

"It's a good thing you came out, Mom. The boys are waterlogged I think." Ben and Ricky were out of the pool and drying off. "Tucker was supposed to meet me up here but he hasn't finished the chores yet. Can I go find him now?"

Rachel told her to go ahead as she helped Ricky towel dry his hair. The boys chatted happily about the pool and all the tricks they could do in the water. Rachel's thoughts were on her other kids. What would Gracie and Danny do? What was the right reaction for her and TJ? What about the other girls? How would they respond?

Rachel got the little guys a snack and tried to concentrate on what they were saying but her mind kept going back to Gracie and then to TJ. She hoped he would be able to sort things out.

"Mama?" She was suddenly aware of Ricky tugging at her arm. "Look!" He pointed at Ben. He had taken his spoon from his pudding and stuck it on his nose. He was trying to see how long it would stay.

Rachel smiled at them. "You are pretty talented there, angel-boy. Can you do it, Ricky?" She grinned at Ricky trying to get his to stay. They were making such funny faces as they concentrated on the trick that Rachel couldn't help but laugh out loud. Then they begged her to try.

"No," she said seriously, "I'm too old to stick spoons on my nose."

"Mama, please!" They both begged, jumping up and down. "Okay, I'll get a spoon and we will see who can walk across the kitchen, spoons on their noses." She got the spoon and she and the boys lined up. "Ready, set, go!" she shouted.

They started walking, heads turned up, laughing. Ricky reached up to grab his spoon as it started to fall. Ben yelled at him to stop cheating. Rachel's spoon slipped and clattered to the floor. She reached to pick it up and rose to see the boys nearly run into TJ who had come in unnoticed and was watching with an amused grin.

"Daddy, you should try this!" Ben told him. "I am the winner though, right Mama? Didn't I win?"

Rachel agreed he was the champion, but she told him she thought it might be all the pudding on his spoon helping it stick. She went to TJ and handed him her spoon.

"Want to have a go?" she asked.

He sighed. "Not particularly in the mood."

He looked into her eyes and she nodded understanding. Smiling down at the boys, she asked them to put their spoons in the dishwasher and go wash their faces. Both had pudding around their mouths and on their noses. They ran down the hall.

TJ gave Rachel a quick embrace. She pulled back a little to study him. His eyes were dark, troubled. She felt the stress come flooding back though she could see he was trying to mask it.

"Hey, want to take a walk with me?" he asked. "I thought maybe the boys could go too and explore while we talk."

"Yes!" Ben yelled excitedly running into the room. "We want to go explore, right Ricky?"

Rachel gave a small shrug. "Guess I'm outnumbered." She

glanced at the clock. "We have a little time." She instructed the boys to go put on socks and shoes. When everyone was ready the group headed out the back door to the trail that led through the holler and back toward the pond.

The boys raced ahead, finding rocks and pinecones, bugs and all kinds of things to show TJ and Rachel. After a couple of interruptions TJ told them the stuff they found was extra special and they couldn't show anyone until the end of the walk.

"Put it in your pocket or keep it hidden, then when the mission is over, we will look at your treasures. But Mama and I need to talk while you find things." The boys agreed and TJ slowed his pace so they could talk quietly while lagging behind the young explorers.

"Rache, I don't know what to say. I can't for the life of me figure out what's the best thing to do. I am so—" TJ shook his head. "I don't know."

"Disappointed?" she suggested.

He nodded.

"In Gracie?"

"Yes. In Danny, too. But also in myself. I feel like I let Kris down somehow. I feel like I let Gracie down, too. I brought that boy around here. Maybe that was a mistake. I should have been more careful. I talked to him about girls and sex. He has come to our camps for kids without dads but I never talked to him specifically about Gracie. I was going to. I should have. I did with Tucker and Naomi but I didn't with Danny and Gracie." He looked so distraught. "Why didn't I see this coming?"

Rachel put her hand on his arm. "It's not your fault, TJ. This was Gracie's and Danny's choice." But even as she said it she knew as a parent she felt guilty as well. And honestly, as much as they considered the kids both of theirs, she knew if it were Naomi, Beth or Emily, she would feel more responsibility and blame.

"I know it, Rachel. But I am still mad I let this happen." He shook his head again. "That's what I mostly feel—angry. I was so furious when I left the house after talking to Gracie and Danny that I wanted to take it out on Tucker, too. I was this close to telling him to get off my property." Rachel looked at him alarmingly. He was usually pretty good at maintaining boundaries when he was upset.

"Don't worry. I didn't do anything. I must have looked pretty outraged cause when Tucker saw my face he actually backed up a step or two. But then he asked if Danny had talked to me. Hell, I should have known we weren't the first ones they told. Danny and Tucker are pretty tight. I guess Danny told him a couple of weeks ago but he made Tucker promise not to tell anyone until they figured out what to do. Emily knows, too. Gracie told her. I guess Naomi and Mary still don't know."

Rachel felt as if the breath had been knocked out of her. She listened to TJ explaining how the kids had struggled with this together. She had assumed Danny had probably talked to Tucker. Danny's mom, according to Gracie, was pretty unstable, and Tucker and Danny were close enough to be brothers. Emily and Gracie were also very close.

"Well, we could have helped more if we had known they were even going out," Rachel finally said. "I can't think straight about it yet. My thoughts are all jumbled. I have no idea what is supportive and what is enabling. Plus, we don't even know what their plans are. But, TJ, do you think it's because we have been so involved with the boys? You know, even before they got here we were totally engrossed in getting ready." She stopped walking and searched his face. "Are we too busy with them?"

"I don't know, Rache. It's tough. There is that slant on it. But the truth is, if kids are going to mess around there's no way to be there to stop it." They resumed their slow walk in silence, each lost in thought. After a few minutes they came upon Ricky and Ben sitting by a large tree looking over their collection.

"Hey, guys!" TJ said as they approached.

"We got tired and had too much stuff to hold," Ben explained.

TJ looked and whispered to Rachel that they could talk later. They both sat with the boys to look over their collections. Maybe they had been preoccupied since the little ones had come. But sitting there, Rachel was thankful for the wholesomeness of the boys' childish thrill over sticks, stones and other bits of nature against the issues that often troubled them and the weighty life issues the older kids faced.

Rachel peered over their heads at TJ who was concentrating on Ben's explanation about the bug he had found. He must have sensed her gaze because he suddenly glanced at her. Their eyes met. TJ smiled. "I love you," he mouthed.

She smiled back. "Me, too."

chapter

As summer's end approached, the crunch to get ready for school closed in on the Keytons. Though Mary was the only one of the girls still in high school, the schedule seemed more hectic than ever with all Rachel had to do for this particular school year. Beth was out on her own. She and Laney had followed through with their plans and found an apartment close to Nashville but the other girls needed her in varying degrees.

TJ had finally persuaded Emily to get some of her education out of the way before pursuing her musical career. She had been pressing him hard so he promised to help her, but only if she agreed to go to school first as originally planned. Seeing he wasn't going to change his mind, she decided to go to Belmont where she had been accepted months earlier. She and Hope would head off to school in a few weeks.

Rachel and TJ had been talking with Heritage Elementary about the boys. When the principal and the school counselor looked over the paperwork they were concerned, especially about Ben's previous behavioral problems. Rachel had hoped since Heritage was a smaller school it would be easier to work as a team and give the boys the individualized attention they would need. Despite the administration's desire to have the Keytons stay with Heritage and TJ's support of the school, the boys' needs seemed to be more than the school could take on. "We just aren't equipped to handle the possible learning and behavioral issues they bring with them," the principal told them honestly. "Even if you bring in your social worker and team of people we have certain standards to adhere to and we aren't set up to accept kids that require the kind of attention we know Ben will need."

Rachel researched schools near Mary's high school that could meet the boys' needs and then, she hoped, they could transfer to Heritage at some point. Lori recommended a public school where one of her other families had good success. The school appeared to be very progressive and innovative in their approach to both education and positive behavioral support. Rachel and TJ were set to talk with them later in the week.

Meanwhile, Gracie and Danny were looking at various options and were still unsure about what they wanted to do. Gracie talked more than once about giving the baby up for adoption and seemed to be leaning that direction. Rachel had to admit, adoption had advantages. It could provide the child with older, more mature parents and would also give Danny and Gracie time to grow up before starting a family. Rachel tried to stay neutral but the truth was it was impossible. This was their kids, their grandchild. All of their lives would be affected by whatever choices were made.

Danny and Gracie were both at dinner the night before. The boys went outside to play while Rachel and TJ talked with the young couple.

"Gracie, Danny, I love you both," TJ said after listening to their views about their options. "I want nothing but the best for both of you. And I honestly don't know what that is at this point. But here's the thing. You all made choices that now include another human being. And part of being a parent is that you have to put that baby's life ahead of your own. What is going to be best for that child?"

Rachel nodded in agreement.

"And here's the other thing. As parents, you are the only ones that can really know what that is. You can look at statistics and get all the advice in the world but from the moment that baby was conceived, he or she was your responsibility. Only you can figure out what is going to best for him or her. No one else can tell you what to do. So look at the options—adoption and otherwise—but above all," TJ said passionately, "I am praying you will be mature enough to put that child's welfare first." He looked to Rachel. "Is there anything you want to add?"

"Danny, Gracie," Rachel said, "most of us around this table have been impacted by choices our parents made because of their own brokenness. We have all been wounded in some way by choices that had nothing to do with what might be best for us as the child. I know you understand this."

The kids listened gravely. They seemed to be taking in all that TJ and Rachel said. Still, they were undecided about what they should do.

Late that night there was a knock on Rachel and TJ's bedroom door. Rachel had been asleep a couple of hours. Waking TJ, she got up to answer and found Gracie crying, asking if she could talk to them. Rachel made room for Gracie on the bed and held her as she began to pour out her heart.

"I just want to say how sorry I am," Gracie sobbed. "I always knew you wanted us to be good girls, Daddy. I guess I thought us being good was part of your reputation or something, like you wanted us to make you look good. I just thought your rule about waiting to have sex was so you could say you did a good job being our daddy. That's what I thought. But I understand so much more now. Daddy, I am sorry. I am so sorry." She was crying too hard to continue.

Rachel rubbed her back. TJ got up and brought a box of tissues from the bathroom. He handed it to Gracie and touched her wet cheek. "Baby—"

Gracie shook her head. "No, Daddy, I have to say this. I never understood all your rules and your values. I think there was this part of me that hated it. And after Mama died, I just got kind of hard in my heart toward God." She paused to blow her nose. "I was doing what you told me, but inside I was fighting all the time. Somewhere along the way I made up my mind I would do things my own way."

She squeezed her eyes tight but tears gushed out anyway. "Now look where I am. I thought all your rules were about controlling us girls. I couldn't see that you wanted what was best for us and just wanted to keep us safe. You provided a way for us to be happy and free. Now I am trapped by my own lies and willfulness. I don't know how to get back to that safe, happy place. It feels like no matter where I go from here my life is ruined."

Gracie reached for another tissue. Rachel could see tears in TJ's eyes and she let her own fall freely. TJ pulled Gracie close and held her. She put her head on his chest and sobbed.

"I am sorry, Daddy. I am so sorry for not trusting you."

She looked to Rachel and motioned for her to join their embrace. The three of them huddled together. Gracie told Rachel, too, that she was sorry. Rachel assured her she loved her no matter what.

"I know, Mama. I know."

Gracie had been the most reluctant of the three girls to allow her a place as mother in her life. Things had been peaceful between them but Rachel never felt Gracie let her close. It was a big moment for both of them.

"Gracie—" TJ cleared his throat, his voice thick with emotion. "—Gracie, we do love you. And because of that love—and I'm sure I speak for Rachel as well—we would love to make all of this better, to wipe it away. But we can't. We can't even provide you with answers about what you and Danny should do. But listen to me. This is the time when you really need Jesus. I know because you're just like me. That battle you have been fighting inside, your biggest battle has really been against God and His plan for you. He is the only one that can give you a clean start, take all of this and turn it into joy. Gracie, I know you know all about Him. But you need to give it all to Him, especially control of your life."

"I know it, Daddy. Danny has been telling me the same thing. I have been feeling so guilty and shameful I find it hard to even pray with him. As soon as we messed up, Danny was asking God to forgive us, but I didn't. I was too stubborn."

"Honey," Rachel said stroking Gracie's curly hair, "He knows all about that. He is the only one that can really forgive and take your shame and guilt. And He already has an answer for you about your future."

"Will you pray with me?" Gracie asked.

The three of them joined hands and Gracie gave her life over to Jesus. And Jesus, already giving His life for her sins, cleansed her heart, took away her shame and gave her new life.

chapter

"I hate you!" Ben yelled at Rachel as he stomped down the hall into his room. "You are so mean!"

Rachel almost followed him, but given her own level of frustration, she thought it best to give them both some space. Exasperated, she folded her arms on the counter and rested her head on them. It had been weeks since the last meltdown but still it felt like a rubber band snapping Ben right back to where they had started.

Although she knew they were making progress, even huge strides at times, this morning felt like a slap in the face. Maybe it was affecting her more today because of all the other stresses—summer ending, school arrangements to be made, the college girls moving out and the uncertainty of Gracie's situation. Usually Rachel could take Ben's behaviors in stride but today it was all she could do to count to ten—and then another ten—without her own attitude interfering with her better judgment.

He had awakened in a foul mood and come into the kitchen demanding that Rachel get him some food. She reminded him to ask politely but he just glared at her, a look she hadn't seen since before camp. He sat at the table in icy silence while Rachel pretended to be busy. After a minute or two he screamed in a voice full of sarcasm, "Hello! I'm hungry!"

Rachel sat across from him and said patiently, "Ben that is not how you get anyone to help you. Would you like to try again?"

She saw trouble brewing in his eyes. She got up and turned away so he wouldn't feel she was challenging him but he slammed his hand down on the table.

"It's not like you don't know I have to eat," he answered defiantly.

Rachel kept her expression neutral and turned to put away the dishes. Detach, detach, detach, she thought. Dr. Anderson had reminded her just last week to remain calm about Ben's need to control his environment. Rachel had experienced this with clients and knew that the more going on inside them the more compelled they felt to try to control everything else. Dr. Anderson was working with Ben on choosing better options. He encouraged TJ and Rachel to allow the boys to earn control through their choices. Dr. Anderson stressed the importance, especially for Ben, to have to give something to get what he wanted rather than constantly demanding and manipulating the environment. By requiring Ben to ask for his breakfast in a polite manner, he got his needs met but also had to give something of himself.

"Ben has a lot of trust issues," he had pointed out after one of their first sessions. "Having to make a request is difficult for him because he equates it with having to admit a need. He would rather do without than have to ask for help. So while we build trust in him that he will be taken care of, we also have to teach him to give in the relationship."

Ben liked having choices and he had come a long way in expressing what he wanted or needed. But not today. The required common courtesy was a price for his breakfast he wasn't willing to pay. Rachel could tell he was determined to go the distance in holding his position.

Still scowling, Ben started kicking the leg of the chair. When that didn't get Rachel's attention, he pounded his fist on the table again. "Give me food now!"

Purposefully avoiding a big reaction or response, Rachel quietly told him to go to his room. "When you are ready to ask properly, come back and I will be happy to help you."

He glared at her, unmoving, undoubtedly plotting his next move.

Rachel told him firmly he had ten seconds to go on his

own or she would walk him. She stood calmly nearby. He seemed to be weighing his options.

"Fine!" he shouted suddenly. He got down from the chair then violently shoved it, knocking it over. With resolve, Rachel placed her hand on his shoulder and elbow and guided him to pick it up. Aggressively, he set it upright, pulled away and stomped out.

Sending Ben to his room was not a "time out" punishment. It was designed to give him space to change his demeanor and immediately try again. Having to sit and stew about what he had done wrong would simply fuel his sense of injustice. Rachel knew that staying calm and offering Ben a way out of the problem by simple compliance was important.

When Ben was not in turmoil Rachel and TJ had been working with him on how to express his anger or other emotions. TJ liked to talk to Ben while they were working on projects and Rachel found walking down to the barn or out to the pond offered great teaching moments. At those times she was able to talk to Ben about how to say what he really felt rather than swearing and spewing hateful words. They wanted him to see alternatives to hurting people with words and actions. Once he started down the path of being hurtful and defiant he had to learn to stop and choose another way.

Over the summer Rachel had seen Ben change directions a few times. During the tantrum it was easy for those working with him to get sidetracked with his behaviors. She had to remind herself to hold steady to what started the conflict and not be distracted with everything else he was doing to draw attention away from the original issue. While she wanted to reprimand him for the words coming out his mouth she had learned that taking on too many of his behaviors at once only led to all out power struggles. On this difficult morning, that meant sticking to the basics of asking politely for breakfast and keeping the routine.

Maybe this would be just a normal temper tantrum, Rachel told herself, knowing how unlikely that would be. Ben's fits were nothing close to the normal category. Still it had been a while since he'd acted out. She prayed it wouldn't last too long or be too many steps backward. Her prayer was interrupted by a large crash. On her way down the hall she prayed softly, "Dear God, please let him be okay."

Ricky already stood at his brother's door. "Ricky, let Mama talk to Ben. Please go potty and then go get one of your sisters to help you with breakfast."

She wished TJ were here but he had left early and wouldn't be back until evening. At first Ricky refused to leave his post by the door. Rachel had to tell him more harshly to do as she said. Not knowing what she would find in the room, she wanted Ricky out of the way. She must have looked fierce because Ricky started crying as he ran down the hall.

"You are hurting my feelings!" He sobbed.

"Ugh," Rachel sighed. She would have to talk to him about that later.

She tried opening the door but whatever had fallen was blocking it. The space was too small for her to squeeze through and she couldn't see into the room. She surmised Ben had pushed his big dresser over. She had no idea how such a small boy had the strength to do it.

"Ben, are you okay?" she called through the crack. She couldn't see him. No answer. "I need you to answer me, Ben. I am worried the dresser has hurt you."

Again, no answer. Rachel listened to hear if he was crying or hurt but she couldn't tell. Near panic, she gave the door a huge shove with her shoulder and it opened a little further. She pushed herself through the opening. She was breathing hard with the effort. Her heart pounded from exertion and worry.

She saw right away that he wasn't under the dresser. That was a relief. But with the relief came a flood of irritation and anger. She fought to control her emotions. Nothing in the room had been destroyed. This would normally be a good thing but as she scanned the room for damages she felt all the more frustrated. Ben sat calmly on his bed complacently watching her fight her way into the room. The look on his face was triumph. He had won by getting her to come to him.

Rachel felt her blood boil. He was fine. He was waiting for her. His haughty, "What are you going to do about it," expression infuriated her. All the words going through her mind were unfit for a child to hear. Every course of action she wanted to pursue involved physical harm. She moved forward and opened her mouth to yell at him but when she saw him physically shrink away the words froze in her throat. She knew he had been hurt so many times and she didn't want to be just another grown-up that brought him pain.

Turning away from the door, she used her anger to help her shove the dresser away. She had no idea the appropriate thing to do about him succeeding at his plan to get her to come to his room. They both knew he had won this battle. It was difficult to focus on what had sent him to his room in the first place. She didn't look at him as she thought about where to go from here.

Once she had moved the dresser she was more composed. "I guess you must be pretty mad to have knocked that dresser over," she said evenly. "We will have to figure out later if it is safe for you to have a dresser in your room."

She stood by the door letting those words sink in. Ben hated having things taken away. Yet having to earn them back made a big difference in how he treated his possessions. Rachel studied him. His prideful look was gone. Her compassion for him returned. He was really just a hurt little boy. "Do you want to talk about what is really bothering you?" she asked gently.

As she suspected, Ben just shrugged. But then his determination returned. "No. I don't want to talk to you!"

"Okay. Suit yourself." Rachel appeared unruffled. She hoped he couldn't tell what a great job he was doing at pushing her buttons. Her mind went back to the kitchen and his refusal to ask politely for his breakfast. Rather than giving something of himself, he did what he had to do to get her to come to him, to notice him. Rachel considered her options. As she thought about the possible reasons for his behavior, she also considered what was in it for Ben. Her mind kept going back to Ben wanting attention. His chosen behavior was not what she wanted to reward. She would ignore this enormous dresser in the middle of the room, she decided, and focus on Ben complying with a simple household rule of respect and courtesy.

Turning to leave, she stuck to the original request. "Ben, when you are ready to start your day over, please come find me and ask for your breakfast." Then she left the room.

Walking into the kitchen she met another disgruntled set of kids. Naomi was making eggs for Ricky. When she saw Rachel, she said irritably, "Mom, this was my only day this week to sleep in. Why did you send him to my room?"

Hearing her remark, Ricky started bawling again. "Everybody's being mean today!"

Rachel didn't know who to start with. Her emotions were still on edge from Ben's behaviors. But Naomi's annoyance and Ricky's tears mixing with her own stress and aggravation pulled her down and threatened to overwhelm her.

"Go back to bed, Naomi," she snapped. "I certainly don't

need your help if it's going to come with a healthy dose of attitude."

Naomi started to protest but Rachel cut her off. "I mean it. Just go."

"Fine." Naomi slammed down the spatula. On her way out she stopped and whispered something in Ricky's ear. Rachel couldn't hear what she said. She hoped it was along the lines of an apology for her grumpiness toward him. Naomi tousled his hair. He looked up at her and nodded his eyes still shiny with tears.

Sighing, Rachel went to the stove and finished the eggs, put them on a plate and set it in front of Ricky. Then she sat down next to him.

"Ricky, Mama's not trying to be mean to you. I know you were worried about Ben, but I needed to talk to him alone." Ricky picked up his fork and pulled his plate closer. He looked at Rachel seriously. "I don't want you to be mad at us." His words were barely audible.

"I'm not mad at you."

"You mad at Omi?" He said it more like a fact than a question. Rachel shook her head.

"You sound mad at us. You told me to go away."

Again Rachel shook her head. "Mama needed to be alone with Ben. Sometimes I need you to listen and do what I say even if it is hard for you." She touched his arm. "Okay?"

"You still mad at Omi and Benny, but not Ricky?" He looked worried. Rachel thought about what it had meant for this little boy when people got upset. Anger at one person or one thing probably splattered on everyone. She had heard enough of his past experiences to know that anger always meant danger even if you weren't the target.

"Ricky, sometimes people get upset, just like you and Ben

get mad with each other, but you still love each other and play together. Mama and Daddy even get angry at each other sometimes. Yes, I was upset with Naomi and Ben, and you, too, when you did not do what I said. But I love you all and that doesn't change."

She wasn't sure how much he understood. He looked uncertain. She decided to change directions. "I am not mad now. I am ready to have a good day. How about you?"

Ricky smiled at her. "Okay, Mama." He started to eat his food. "You should tell Omi sorry too." Rachel looked at him as he ate hungrily. Then she laughed out loud. He was right. "Okay, Baby. I will." From the mouth of babes, she thought as she went upstairs to apologize to Naomi for being so sharp with her.

Naomi apologized for her attitude. "Mom, things are just really weird right now, you know? All this stuff is just so crazy, like Gracie and Danny and just not knowing what is going to happen. Plus everyone is moving out and I feel like I can't talk about it with anyone. Tucker is worried about Danny and doesn't want to tell me anything. We even got into a big fight about it. It's okay now but— And then you and Dad are so busy with the boys and getting ready for school. Seems like everyone is getting ready for something and it feels like I'm the only one not going anywhere. Since it looks like there is nothing going on with me everyone just thinks I am fine, you know?"

Rachel felt guilty. She knew Naomi was right. It was easy to focus on the ones who were obviously struggling or whose needs were glaring. Even though she felt bad for Naomi, Rachel was overwhelmed. There was always someone not getting enough of her. Pushing down the inner turmoil, she forced herself to focus on what Naomi was saying.

"I'm sorry, Naomi. It sounds like you are feeling alone and

unsure in all the upheaval. I have been pretty busy dealing with immediate issues but I do want to talk to you, too. It must seem like I never will have enough time. I know it feels like that to me."

"Well, honestly," Naomi said, "I can tell you are really stressed out. I want to help, not make it worse for you. I just feel kind of invisible though."

"I do really appreciate your help, Naomi. You are so good with the boys. And you are good to your sisters, too. I probably haven't thanked you nearly enough."

"No, you haven't," Naomi said jokingly. She held out her hand teasingly. "You can thank me with payback."

Rachel took her hand. "How about we take a day, once we get everyone back in school, and I show my appreciation with shopping and lunch?"

"I would like that," Naomi said.

"Me, too. I miss being able to visit with you." Rachel stood to leave. "I have to go and see about Ben now. He's having a bad morning."

"Got that loud and clear even from up here," Naomi said.

"Mom, you probably already know this but all this craziness is probably not helping Ben's behavior."

"I am sure you're right," Rachel agreed. Just one more thing she couldn't fix.

Coming downstairs and back into the kitchen, she was surprised that Ben was not waiting for his breakfast. Ricky had already finished and left the table, his chair and plate empty. She figured he had probably gone to be with Ben. It was difficult to keep them apart. When one was in trouble they became all the more inseparable. She peeked into Ricky's room. Empty. So she went to check Ben's. At the door she heard the happy sounds of boyish play as their imaginations took them to other places.

She hated to bring their exchange to an end but she reminded herself that parenting wasn't about keeping the peace. "Hey guys." She stepped casually into the room and sat on the bed. "What is the game?"

Ben had apparently forgotten he was supposed to be upset. He and Ricky both filled her in with enthusiasm.

"Wow! Sounds like a lot of fun," Rachel said cheerfully. "Maybe you can leave it right here and get back to it as soon as we take care of morning chores."

"Nooo, please Mama, chores later," Ricky whined. Rachel shook her head. The morning had had enough interruptions. She and TJ had agreed on the structure of the schedule for the boys. They had both noticed the benefits of holding them to the routine, especially on days like today.

"Ricky, you need to go back to the kitchen and put your breakfast dishes away. Then you can look at your chart and see what you need to do. Ben?" She looked at her older son. He was fiddling with a toy truck. "Did you eat breakfast yet?" she asked, knowing, of course, he hadn't. She wanted to give him a fresh start. She hoped he was willing. She tried to read his face but he kept his head down. Uh-oh, she thought. He was weighing his options. She needed to narrow the choices.

"I am going to cook up some eggs and toast," she informed him. "They will be ready soon. If you decide you want to eat I will have them on the table. If you don't want breakfast today that is okay. You can go ahead and get started on your chart." She held out her hand to Ricky and led him to the chore chart in his room.

"No playing until you both finish your morning chores," she instructed firmly despite his whining protests. "I mean it, Ricky. When you are done come get me so I can put the

stickers on your chart. You need to let Ben do his jobs, too."
Rachel went into the kitchen, prepared the food for Ben and
put it on the table. Taking a cup of coffee, she went into her
room. Lord, help us, she thought as she picked up her Bible
and journal. She kept her door open so she could hear what
was going on down the hall.

The roller coaster of emotions continued throughout the
morning. It was one of their last days of summer and despite
Rachel's best efforts to make it go smoothly things kept
twisting out of control. By midday, stress sat solidly on Rachel's
shoulders. Ben continued to be edgy, which seemed to make
Ricky all the more clingy and needy.

Pressing on Rachel's mind were all the things she needed
to do for the boys and wondering if she was letting the other
kids down. She was concerned about Naomi feeling invisible,
Emily wanting to go over plans to develop her music career
and Beth asking for help setting up her classroom. It was one
of those days when every step forward felt like walking in waist-
high water.

By the time TJ and Emily got home from their meeting
with a Nashville producer that evening, Rachel felt utterly
drained. Not only that, despite her efforts to the contrary, it
annoyed her that he had agreed to take her when they had
decided she would go to school first. Rachel listened to Emily
talk excitedly about career possibilities but inside she felt
irritated.

She didn't voice her complaints because she didn't want to
dampen Emily's spirit or her dreams. Emily and TJ had such
energy, energy Rachel couldn't muster. She felt betrayed that
they had had such a good day.

The boys danced around TJ. It seemed the whole kitchen
buzzed with excitement. Usually Rachel loved times like this

but her head felt foggy. She felt inexplicably close to tears.

The little ones begged TJ to come play with them. Emily rushed off to call some of the guys in her band. Rachel turned away to get water boiling for dinner. TJ came up behind her, put his hand on her shoulder and moved her to face him. "What's up, Babe? You look wiped."

"It was been a really hard day, TJ. I can't seem to catch up." The boys crowded around them vying for TJ's attention. He told them to go get their swimsuits on and he would take them out for a bit before supper. They raced to their rooms.

TJ pulled Rachel close. Though she didn't intend to, she stiffened a bit. "What?" he asked.

"Why are you getting Emily all excited about the music stuff again?" Rachel felt testiness creep into her voice. "I thought we had a deal with her about school."

"We do have a deal. Doesn't mean she has to kill her desire though. Besides, she is way more excited than is warranted for what we did today."

They were quiet for a moment. Rachel wasn't sure all what was bothering her had that much to do with this common argument about Emily and the music business. What really was wrong with her?

The boys bounded in saying they were ready to go out. TJ gave Rachel a concerned look. "I'll take the kids," he said.

Rachel knew he was trying to help, thinking she probably needed time alone. He lifted her chin and gave her a gentle kiss. "I love you," he said reassuringly.

"I know. I love you, too. It's just—been—a day." She tried to smile. "Better take those boys. I'll be okay." As he followed Ben and Ricky outside, Rachel turned back to the task at hand. Suddenly alone as she prepared dinner, tears stung and she tried to swallow the great lump in her throat. She hooked up her iPod to the kitchen stereo and chose some uplifting music.

Rachel had started to feel a little better when Gracie came home with Danny. They exchanged greetings then Danny went out to see what TJ and boys were doing. Gracie stayed in the kitchen and set the table. She was starting to show a little and in spite of everything Rachel thought she looked absolutely beautiful. Since that night she had given everything over to God Gracie seemed to glow. She appeared more peaceful than Rachel had ever seen her.

While they placed bowls of food on the table Rachel reminded her she had a doctor appointment the following week.

"Will they do an ultrasound?" Gracie asked.

"Yes. They will want to make sure how far along you are."

"Danny and I decided to wait to make a decision until after that appointment," Gracie said quietly. "We don't want to know if it is a boy or girl but we want you and Dad both to be there."

"Gracie, we want to be there," Rachel told her reassuringly, patting her arm. She felt close to tears again but pulled herself together. "Can you get Naomi and Emily from upstairs?"

Gracie gave her a quick hug and went up to get her sisters. Rachel called the guys in from the pool. Just as they were getting settled at the table, Beth called. "Hey, Mom, I know you are probably getting ready to eat."

"Hi, Beth, what's up?"

"Laney and I are heading over to the Metcafes for the evening. Aunt Tina said I should call you and tell you all to come over for dessert and a visit. Should I tell them you will come?"

Rachel put her hand over the phone and quietly asked TJ. He nodded.

"Sure, Hon, tell them we will be there after dinner."

Rachel figured it would be good to get away from the farm and be around other adults. She expected everyone to jump at the chance to spend the evening out.

"Do we have to go?" Naomi asked.

"I am kind of surprised you don't want to," Rachel commented. "You usually want to go."

"Tucker's coming over and we were talking about going to a movie or something."

"Well, call him and tell him to meet you at the Metcafes," TJ said matter-of-factly.

"Do we have to?" Naomi nearly whined.

TJ shrugged. "I don't know, Rache, do they have to?" He gave a sort-of laugh.

Rachel wondered why everything had to be so complicated. She missed the days when they decided what they were doing and everyone got in the suburban and went. She sighed. "I think it would be better if you guys hung out with everyone. You know you can't be here alone and it would just be better if you came, don't you think?"

Naomi hesitantly agreed. Danny and Gracie said they would go and encouraged Naomi to call Tucker and they could ride over together. Naomi looked unsure.

Emily was happy about the plans. She wanted to tell everyone about her day in Nashville. She called Hope and asked her to meet them after she got off work. The boys were eager as well to go to "Aunt Tina's and Uncle Mike's."

"Can we swim there, too, Mama?" Ben asked.

"Hmm. I'm not sure. Maybe we could pack your swimsuits and your jammies, too, in case we stay late."

"And my toothbrush," Ricky said.

TJ grinned at her. Rachel smiled back but inside she was tired. She realized she wanted the kids all in one place so she could relax and not wonder where they were or if they were okay. She looked forward to just being able to visit with Tina and Mike.

Once they finished dinner Rachel started to clear the table. TJ rose and took the dishes from her hands. "I'll do this, Rache," he said. "Why don't you go get the boys ready to go." He pointed at Ricky, Ben and Danny. "Come on, men, let's clean up the kitchen." Rachel thanked him and kissed his cheek.

On the way to the Metcafes Rachel quietly filled TJ in on her day with Ben. Rachel tried to explain how overwhelmed she felt with the kids and everything else.

"I couldn't figure out anything today. It just seemed like one thing after another. I left the stupid dresser in the middle of the floor."

TJ said he would move it out of the room and they could put his clothes in the closet. "No big deal, Rache," he added. "If we have to empty the room, that's what we'll do. You know that though. Heck, you're the one that told me that." He reached over and held her hand. "You're tired."

"I know it. I feel restless though. So much stuff going on."

They pulled into the Metcafe's drive. Rachel loved their ranch. She had stayed there with her kids when she first met TJ. It always seemed like home. The boys, once released from the car seats, went running up to the door, pushing each other to be first to ring the doorbell.

Danny and Gracie, Tucker and Naomi pulled into the drive just as Rachel and TJ were going in. Rachel was thankful they came. Technically, they were all adults and could do what they wanted. It did her heart good to know where they all were. It seemed less stressful.

"I know," TJ said, apparently reading her thoughts. "I'm relieved having them all here, too."

It was like old times—Rachel, TJ, Mike and Tina in the hot tub. The boys had fallen asleep watching a movie in the guestroom. The older kids were all playing a board game together. Rachel could hear them inside the house laughing.

She and Tina chatted about the kids and who was doing what. Tina asked about Gracie and Danny. Rachel caught her up to speed. Together they tried to imagine what Gracie would decide to do and what it would be like.

"I don't know how you are holding up, Rache, but you are definitely my hero. I would have killed at least one of them by now."

Rachel chuckled. "I thought you and Mike were the heroes. You guys have the perfect family—no teenage pregnancies, no wild boys or anything like that."

Mike overheard her. "Listen, Cowgirl, better just watch what you say. What you have might be catching."

"Someday we will all look back on this, you know," TJ added, "and laugh nervously and change the subject."

"Well, one thing for sure," Tina said. "If it is catching at least we will know how to handle it, thanks to you guys."

"Yeah, if it were only as easy as we apparently make it look!" Rachel suddenly felt weary again. Maybe it was the warm water, or just being with good friends, feeling safe and loved. Whatever it was, the emotions she had held back all day came over her like a flood. Before she could stop, she was crying. She confessed how difficult the day had been; how she constantly felt close to failing and how uncertain she was what to do or how to react. It poured out of her how badly she felt about Gracie and how worried she was about Naomi and Tucker and whether they, too, were headed for trouble. The words and the tears rushed out.

Her friends were great. They let her cry and vent and offered little in the way of advice or empty sympathy. When the torrent slowed, she quipped, "How's that for having it all together?" She was slightly embarrassed and cursed herself. "Damn."

"Oh, Rache," Tina said, "I'm glad you know you don't have to have it all together around us. What a blessing."

Mike agreed with her.

Rachel looked at TJ. He hadn't said anything. She wondered if he was humiliated by her behavior. She herself was trying to decide if she felt relieved or mortified. Leaning back in the hot tub, TJ stared up into the night sky so Rachel couldn't read his face. He must have sensed her waiting for his response. He turned to her and then to their friends quietly watching the two of them. He scooted closer and put his arm around her. She leaned against him.

"Well," he said, "I'll admit it has been busy and complicated at our place this summer. We have no idea what will happen with the boys this fall at school or what the next step is for Gracie and Danny. I guess I have been so caught up in trying to keep my own stupid head above water I had no idea Rachel was feeling like this." He squeezed her in a little tighter. "I feel kind of foolish actually for not paying more attention."

"Sounds like the two of you could use some time without kids," Tina said. "At least a day or two. When was your last downtime?"

"We each have time throughout the week to ourselves but not together," Rachel confided. "Even time like this with friends is rare these days."

"Well, shoot, why don't you all let us have the boys for the next few days?" Mike nearly demanded. "The other kids can stay here, too, for that matter."

"Like old times," Tina said smiling.

"Really?" Rachel looked at TJ. "What do you think?"

"Do you think the world will unravel if we let go for a while and escape together?" he teased, but Rachel knew what he meant. She admitted it felt like everything was being held together by sheer willpower. If they let one thing drop they might lose everything.

"Well," Mike jumped in, "if you all think you're what's keeping everything together you need the time away even more than I thought."

TJ and Rachel both turned and looked at him, knowing he had more to say. Mike had a way of cutting through all the crap and saying what needed to be said. Rachel had learned to pay attention when he did that.

"Listen, you all need our proven sage advice here." He pointed at the both of them. "Tina and I decided something a long time ago. It has helped us in the worse of storms." He paused for effect. "Want to hear it?"

Rachel nodded. She sure did. She could feel TJ tense beside her. She knew he had a hard time when Mike got parental like this. She put her hand on his leg to restrain him. "Go ahead, and tell us."

"If it looks like the ship is sinking—" Mike paused for dramatic effect. "—Tina and I get in the life raft."

Everyone was perfectly still, not saying a thing as the words hung in night air. Rachel was thinking it had to be a joke, but Mike's expression never changed and Tina looked just as serious.

"What?" TJ laughed, confused.

"Think about it." Mike pointed at the two of them again. "Your daughter is pregnant. Your other kids are in the process of moving out and going every which way. Your boys are two little hellions that have their own agendas for survival. The only sure thing is that you got into this ship because you love each other. You may think baling water out by the bucket load is keeping you all afloat, but it isn't."

"It's your love," Tina chimed in. "Get in the life raft."

Rachel laughed, shaking her head. "You guys. Seriously. That's it? The ship may be sinking; get in the life raft?"

"Yep," Mike nodded.

"Wow." Rachel looked at TJ. He was staring at Mike. Then he broke into a huge grin. Taking Rachel's hand, he said to Mike, "You're right." Then turning to Rachel, he said, "Hey Baby, want to get in the life raft with me?"

"Of course," she said. "I'd go anywhere with you."

Mike and Tina smiled and told them to go on home then. They would call in the morning to see what the plans were.

"Meanwhile," Tina said, "we got the boys. And we are fine."

So TJ and Rachel gathered their things, left all the kids behind and drove to their house. It seemed so big and quiet. Rachel tried to think of a time they had ever been home late at night alone. She didn't think it had ever happened before. After checking on the dogs and turning off the lights, Rachel went into the master bedroom to get ready for bed.

"Hey, Babe." TJ came up behind her and softly nuzzled her ear. His arms wrapped around her waist and his breath warmed her neck. "I'm sorry." She turned around in his arms so she could see his face.

"TJ, I was never upset at you. I think I just needed to unload it all, you know? It was a lot to carry around."

He touched her face, moving her hair away from her eyes. "No, I'm sorry I haven't tried to set some time for just us. I used to be good at this kind of thing. I knew we needed it. I just kept letting everything else get in the way."

"It's been hard to even think about leaving the boys. We knew it was going to be like this for at least the first year. But I haven't felt unloved or anything. And yes, you used to be quite good at coming up with little get-a-ways and surprises.

Do you think you've still got it?"

"Oh, Baby." He swaggered and swayed against her. "I still got it." He kissed her sweetly.

As tired as she was, his kisses held the power to make her forget all about sleep. He led her to the bed and covered her with his body and his affection. Rachel felt wrapped in love, drifting out to sea.

"TJ," she whispered with a sigh of deep satisfaction, "this is the life raft, isn't it?"

He murmured his agreement.

chapter

The first day of their mini-vacation they simply spent time in the house together and made the necessary arrangements to go away for a few days. It had been a while since Rachel and TJ had even thought about going anywhere. The time was precious. Once they had things in order, TJ told Rachel to pack because he had a surprise for her.

She had put things in a suitcase for the boys, rearranged her schedule, and called the girls about taking care of things while they were gone. TJ had made arrangements for them to fly to North Carolina to the Outer Banks.

Rachel had always wanted to see the wild horses of Shackleford Banks. For two days they walked the beaches, watched the horses, explored the low tides and spent time talking, making love and just being together. When they got back they would have to hit the ground running but Rachel felt refreshed and ready to handle it.

The boys had fared pretty well. There were a few bumps in the road but no big meltdowns. The first two days they had stayed with Tina and Mike then Naomi took them home on her day off to get resettled for Rachel and TJ's return. There had been tears from Ricky the first night, but Mike and Tina kept reassuring both boys their mama and daddy were coming back. Ben got a little insolent the last day, pushing the limits. Mike, with his no nonsense attitude, had Ben pal around the ranch with him and took him on a few errands. Rachel was relieved they had done alright.

Back at home, there were conflicts as the boys settled back into the routine. Ben came home to a nearly empty room. His dresser had been removed as well as all other heavy objects. TJ patiently explained to him that he could earn those things back but until he could control his anger they had to do what they could to keep him safe. He followed up with Ben on ways to express himself so he could have his things back quickly. Rachel thought the room resembled a prison cell but she knew Dr. Anderson would approve their course of action.

The first day home, the boys had counseling appointments and Gracie had her ultrasound. Rachel and TJ were needed for both. Afterward they planned to meet back at the house. Danny had asked for his mom to come by so they could discuss future plans.

"Hey, Rache." TJ pulled her aside while the boys did their morning chores and Emily put the dishes away. "Do you have a minute?"

"No," she said half-jokingly. "But I'll shuffle other minutes around to make some for you."

His eyes were serious. "That would be great."

Rachel asked Emily to give the boys instructions as needed and when their chores were done they could pick a movie to watch.

"The movie is for after she puts the stickers on your chart," Rachel explained to the boys. She handed Emily the stickers and headed to the bedroom with TJ.

He closed the door and took a deep breath, then just looked at her.

"Hon, you're making me really nervous," Rachel said. "What's going on?"

"Danny came on my run with me this morning." TJ hesitated and then said plainly, "He asked if he could marry Gracie."

"Well," Rachel paused, "we knew this was coming or at least that it was a possibility."

"I know."

"What did you tell him?"

TJ shook his head. "I didn't tell him one way or another.

I asked him how he was going to do that. And I asked him if he was going to do it even if I disagreed. He said he hadn't asked Gracie yet because he wanted to know what I thought first." TJ rubbed his chin and shook his head again. "I told him I wasn't sure getting married was going to make everything alright. What do you think?"

"TJ, I don't know. In the end, they have to decide."

"I know it. But I think they really want to know where we stand. Anyway, I told him I thought someone ready to get married should have a way to provide for his family, a place to live, and hopefully something for the future. He agreed, but—"

"But they are having a baby together," Rachel said simply.

"Exactly." TJ sat on the bed.

"I have never agreed with people getting married to cover up one mistake. Seems like a set up for a series of others." Rachel sat next to him. "On the other hand, if they are going to keep this baby how do we not do what we can to help them be as stable as possible for the child? Did he say how he thinks he can do this?"

"He said he didn't have it all worked out. He just wanted to know what I thought about them getting married. The thing I keep realizing is that those kids know they screwed up. I know they need and want our help to figure things out. It really hit me this morning that Danny is just a kid, but he is a good kid. And more than anything he wants to make things right. If we don't know the right thing to do, think how confusing it is for them. I know we have tried to be supportive without telling them what to do one way or another but after Danny left this morning I just keep thinking that what they are really asking is for us to get involved. They don't just want our advice, they want our help and I think we're going to have to help them to make it work."

As Rachel reflected on this her mind went back to her mother telling her from the time she was a young teen, "If you get pregnant I am not going to help raise your babies." At the time, and even now, it never made sense to her. As an adult she could see that perhaps it was to warn her against becoming sexually active, which she wasn't, but the message Rachel got was that if she made a mistake she was on her own. And she understood her mother clearly didn't want to have to raise grandkids. As it turned out, she had nothing to do with Rachel's girls.

Now as a mother herself, Rachel couldn't imagine saying or implying anything like that to any of their kids. Wasn't it to some extent the responsibility of the older generation to help raise the younger? Even if Gracie were older, wouldn't Rachel want to be a part of this? Wouldn't she and TJ do everything they could to help their kids keep their families strong and healthy?

TJ watched her face as Rachel contemplated this. "What are you thinking?" he finally asked.

"I'm thinking you're right. We do have a position of honor to uphold here. The kids have invited us to step in and help. I am not sure what that looks like. Maybe we just have to be willing to be involved rather than waiting on the sidelines to see what they decide."

There was a knock on the door. It was Emily. "Mom, the boys are watching their movie. I gotta go with Hope to get some stuff for my dorm room."

Rachel thanked her for helping out and gave her a hug. Turning back to TJ, they resolved to hear the kids out today and be open to how God would have them be a part of whatever they decided.

"Just so you know, before Danny left this morning I told him I really appreciated him talking to me. I think he knows

I will stand by them no matter what. Hey, Rache, I know we both have things we need to do to get ready for today. But do you want to pray with me?"

They knelt by the bed and asked Jesus to help them to parent with His heart. TJ prayed for Danny to have wisdom. Rachel prayed for the baby and the time they would all have together today as they saw this new little one for the first time through the ultrasound.

When they were done Rachel got the boys ready for their counseling appointments. She and TJ planned to bring them back home afterward to hang out with Beth until Rachel and TJ got back from Gracie's doctor appointment.

That afternoon Danny, Naomi, Rachel, and TJ crowded into the small room where Gracie lay on the metal table with her belly exposed ready for the ultrasound. The doctor squirted the cold gel on Gracie's tummy. TJ leaned close to Rachel and said quietly, "Doesn't seem like that long ago I was here with Kris watching Gracie on that screen."

"I know, right?" Rachel agreed thinking back on her own pregnancies.

"Okay, Gracie, we are here to get measurements to confirm your due date and make sure everything is alright." He addressed Gracie and Danny but also looked over at TJ and Rachel. "Are there any concerns? And do we want to know the sex of the baby?"

"Not yet." Gracie was firm in her decision despite pleas from Naomi. "Maybe at the next one."

"Just as well. We will be more certain then. Okay, let's get started."

The group clustered together watching the little image on the screen. When they were done Gracie had a DVD of the ultrasound and a printed picture of the baby.

Everything appeared normal and the due date was set for the end of February.

While the kids walked ahead in the parking lot, TJ took hold of Rachel's hand. They talked about seeing the baby. She smiled up at TJ. Again she was struck by how beautiful Gracie looked. She was dying to know what Gracie was thinking and feeling. "Babe, I know this whole thing is crazy and not what we planned for our kids but she looks absolutely radiant."

TJ looked at Gracie and smiled agreement. "She reminds me most of Kris, at least to look at her."

The kids got into their car. TJ waved and hollered at them to drive safely.

"She may look like Kris," Rachel replied, "but she reminds me most of you."

"Uh-oh. That bad, huh?" he joked. "What part? Her charm? Her spunk? Her smarts?" He laughed and slid into the passenger side of Rachel's '66 Mustang.

"No, I think it's your stubbornness." She grinned at him. "Oh, and thanks for letting me drive the 'Stang." TJ had given her the convertible their first Christmas together. He claimed to hate Fords and said he would never buy one but he knew for ages she had wanted a classic Mustang. He tracked down the one her grandmother had owned, bought it and restored it to surprise her. Rachel hardly ever got to drive it though since they usually took one of TJ's cars or the SUV.

"See, I'm not that stubborn. I'm being driven around in a Ford by a woman."

"Wow! If I didn't know you better I would think you were chauvinistic."

"Not chauvinistic, Babe. It's just at the end of the day, I'm still a guy."

"Well, we may not agree on cars but you are damn straight

about that." Rachel beamed at him and snickered.

Back at home they had about an hour before their meeting with Gracie and Danny. Rachel sought out the boys. They were in the pool with Beth, Emily and Mary. Rachel sat by the edge while the boys splashed and showed her the new game Beth had taught them. It felt good to cool off. Rachel thought about getting her suit on but decided there wasn't enough time.

"Mama! Watch me!" Ricky learned to swim underwater this summer and was constantly demanding that she watch. Beth came over and sat next to her. Both dangled their legs in the water.

"How did it go?" Beth asked.

Rachel told her about seeing the baby's image and how everything was on target.

"Do you know what they are going to do?"

"Not yet. I think they may let us know in about an hour. Can you stay longer, watch the boys and then have supper with us?"

"Only if you promise to come to school with me later this week and help me set up my classroom."

Laughingly, Rachel agreed. "How were the boys?"

"You know, they do alright with people they don't know very well. I think Ricky's missing you though. He asked about you at least half a dozen times in the last hour. Ben's been a handful but once he figured out I already knew all the rules, he decided to relax." Beth laughed. "I can see where he will be tricky in a classroom. He can be quite the charmer until he doesn't get what he wants."

"You don't know the half of it. He goes from zero to full blown faster than a New York minute. It can get intense extremely quickly."

"I could see that. I had to send him to his room a couple of times. He almost didn't get to come out to swim. Did you talk to the school yet?"

"We have an appointment Monday. So far we've done everything via email and phone calls. But Lori thinks this school will work with us to handle Ben's needs. Monday we'll go over his IEP. I want it changed from his previous one. I am bringing in Dr. Anderson so if they want to put me in the overactive mom category at least they'll have another expert to listen to."

"Well, it might go well, you know. That school has a good reputation."

"It might," Rachel conceded.

"Is Ricky going to have an IEP too?"

"That is the million dollar question. Lori thinks we should see how he does with the regular work and classroom first. He is a little delayed in speech, at least he was in the spring, but he may be caught up now. I think we are going to give it a go without it and then talk about it at parent-teacher conferences in the fall."

TJ came out the patio door. "Hey, Rache, Gracie and Danny are here." He waved to Beth. "Hi, girl. How are you?" He walked over to give her a hug and to say hello to the kids in the pool.

"Daddy!" The boys shouted for TJ to watch their new tricks and begged him to get in the water with them.

"I can't right now, guys. But tell you what. How about I cook up some burgers later and we swim together after dinner? Maybe Mama will swim with us."

Rachel nodded to seal the bargain.

"Sounds like a swim party," Emily called to the boys over their continued pleadings for TJ to join them. "If we wait, both Mama and Daddy will swim with us. In fact, maybe we should get out for now so we can get back in later."

Beth agreed. "Hey, guys, I still haven't been down to say hi to the horses. Will you boys take me?"

Rachel inaudibly thanked the girls as she slipped back inside the house behind TJ. She poured a glass of sweet tea and took it out to Beth before going in to talk with Danny and Gracie.

When Danny's mom arrived the small group of adults looked at Gracie and Danny expectantly. They had passed around the picture of the baby from the ultrasound. Danny stood next to Gracie who sat fiddling with her hands the way Rachel had seen TJ do a million times.

Danny looked at TJ who gave him a nod to go ahead.

"Um, as you know, Gracie and I have been trying to figure out what we should do. Before we tell you our plans there are some things I have to say. I guess the main thing is that Gracie having this baby has changed our lives, our plans and our relationship. When we first found out I thought I had ruined my life, and hers. But what Gracie and I want to tell you is that it hasn't screwed our lives up like we thought." Danny spoke passionately from his heart. "I am not saying what we did was right but what has happened to us since then has changed us. All of this has made us really think through our choices and think outside of our own selfishness."

Rachel listened, fascinated by the young man who seemed to be growing up in front of her. TJ reached over, took her hand and gave her a reassuring smile that seemed to say he knew what was coming and it was going to be okay.

"We don't have every detail planned out, so I am not going to pretend we know what we are doing," Danny continued, "but we have prayed a lot and we are doing what we think is the right thing for both of us and for this baby." Danny didn't look at any of them as he spoke. He kept his eyes on Gracie. "We feel the right thing is for us to keep the baby."

Rachel felt her breath catch. She couldn't identify the mix of emotions. Danny stood uncomfortably, now searching their faces. She saw in Danny's eyes a mix of joy and uncertainty. She saw both in TJ as well.

"Please, Danny, have a seat," TJ said evenly.

Rachel slowly exhaled as Danny sat down. The air was silent and tense for a moment. Then Gracie started talking. "I just want to say that keeping the baby was not an easy decision. Both Danny and I had other plans for our futures. We did a lot of thinking and praying, especially about what you said, Daddy—that we had to put the baby first. Initially, I thought it was obvious that the best thing for the baby was to give it to people who were older and could be a real family for him or her. But when I really gave my own heart and life over to Jesus it started changing for me. I told Danny I didn't know how we were going to do it but that I really felt like Jesus wanted us to keep this baby in this family. He started showing me that His plan for my life was different from mine." Gracie paused and looked at each person, her eyes glistening with tears as she recounted the spiritual and emotional battle she had been fighting.

"Danny and I have been praying about all of it," she reiterated. "Sometimes the bravest and most difficult thing to do is to ask for help and not try to solve it all your own way. We wanted you to be here because we know the right next step is to have this baby and for me to keep her, or him, but we don't know the steps after that."

"I do, Gracie," Danny spoke softly but with quiet confidence. "At least I know this." He glanced quickly at TJ. "I realize it doesn't make sense—that it should be better planned— but I have to go with what I do know. Gracie, I want to and I believe God wants me to commit my life to you. He doesn't want me to leave this child fatherless." Danny got down on one knee in front of Gracie. "We have a lot to work out, and I'm not sure when or how, but will you marry me?"

Gracie looked over at her dad. He smiled and gave her a nod. Rachel felt tears on her cheeks as Gracie got up from her chair. Danny stood too, and Gracie wordlessly put her arms around his neck.

TJ went to Danny and put clasped his shoulder. "I would take that as a yes, Son." He patted Danny's back. Gracie let go of Danny and hugged her dad.

Rachel knew that if they hadn't talked and prayed that morning this moment might have been completely different. She thanked God for His timing.

After the hugs and congratulations TJ asked the kids to sit down so they could talk through a few things. TJ told them he had been thinking and praying a lot, too, and that Gracie and Danny had taught him some things. One was that growing up didn't necessarily happen because you figured everything out your own. And another was that being a family was a lifelong thing.

"We didn't want to interfere and we didn't want to give you a way out of your responsibility. But after we talked this morning, Danny, I realized that part of being a family is that we all need each other—sometimes to lean on, sometimes to be carried and sometimes to be pushed. Rachel and I want you to know we are all in this all the way, together, wherever that takes us."

"I really appreciate that, Sir," Danny nodded. "I know none of this has been easy for you guys."

"There is still a lot that makes this not easy," TJ confirmed, "but I think it is right that we struggle through it together, don't you, Rache?"

"Yes, I do. It seems God is doing something here, in all of us."

TJ put his hand out to shake Danny's and then pulled him into a quick embrace. "And we will talk about those next steps, okay? There are many things to put on the table and consider." TJ stepped back and peeked at his watch.

"But right now I have to go cook hamburgers because I promised two little guys I would BBQ tonight before a swim party. So since I'm teaching my sons to be men of their word, I have to go." He embraced Gracie again and winked at Rachel. "You all are staying to swim tonight, right?" he asked heading for the door. "Need to know how many burgers I should throw on the grill. Rache, can you get a count?"

"Yep, right behind you." She gave Gracie and Danny a hug. "I am proud of you and love you both."

After giving TJ an approximate burger count, Rachel decided to walk down to the barn where the boys were hanging out with Beth. On her way she reflected on how life was always changing, turning and twisting on you. Sudden surprises interrupted endless days of the most basic stuff. She thought about the changes she had seen in Gracie as God worked from the inside out. She remembered what Dr. Anderson had said about noticing and celebrating small steps and little changes in the boys.

Ben and Ricky wanted Rachel to give all the horses near the fence some more carrots. Rachel asked the boys how many the horses had already had.

Ricky looked at her solemnly. "Only two or six or five maybe."

Rachel laughed. "Maybe five?"

"Mama, Tracker is a bad horse," Ben interrupted. "He ate all the carrots and he won't let Shy Girl have any!"

Rachel was amused that Ben was all about fairness and making things even. If he had to follow the rules he wanted everyone else to also. She heard the frustration in his voice and wondered how he had handled it. She didn't have to wonder long.

"Yes, but that doesn't mean you can hit him," Beth said to Ben. Looking over at Rachel, she gave her a meaningful nod.

"Right, Mom?"

"Come here, Ben and Ricky." Rachel took the boys over to Tracker and showed them a scar that ran under his forelock. Then she showed them other scars, one under his mane and another on his back hip. "When I got Tracker he had been hurt really badly. He wouldn't let me touch his head or give him a hug like he does now. He was afraid that everyone was mad at him." Rachel watched Ben as he softly fingered the scar on Tracker's neck. Tracker put his head low as if he understood he was part of an important teaching moment. "I had to be really careful and move very slowly or he would think I was going to hurt him. And when he thought he was going to get hurt he acted like he didn't want anyone around him. So he would push me away with his head or put his ears back. It took a long time for Tracker to realize there would always be enough food and love to go around and that no one was going to hurt him." Rachel scratched Tracker's neck while the boys stood quietly.

"That's what happened to me," Ben said softly. "See?" He pushed his hair aside and exposed a faint scar on his forehead. "I asked my other mama to get me some milk." His voice dropped so low Rachel had to strain to hear him. It was the first time he had willingly told her anything about his biological mother. "She threw the glass at me and told me to get it myself." Ben cried quietly.

Rachel knelt beside him and touched the scar the same way he had touched Tracker's. "That must have hurt a lot," she said softly.

"I–I don't remember."

His tear-filled eyes locked on hers. She felt them water as well.

"One time she threw me at the wall." He went back to petting Tracker. He said to the horse or maybe to himself, "At least you are too big for anyone to throw you."

Tracker turned his head toward Ben and nuzzled his hair, which made Ben laugh. "I think he wants to see my scar, too!"

"Maybe," Rachel agreed. "Maybe he wants you to know he understands."

Ben reached his little arms around Tracker's neck as far as he could. Rachel heard him tell Tracker, "I understand."

Rachel looked over Tracker's back to Beth who also had tears in her eyes. Ricky had moved over to Shy Girl and seemed to have missed most of the conversation. Even with all the counseling sessions, Ben usually volunteered very little about what had happened to him. Telling her this story and connecting with Tracker in this way was a huge step. Rachel whispered to Beth, "Therapists in horse hair," and winked at her. "Didn't I tell you they were the best?" To the boys she said, "Come on guys. We need to head to the house. Your daddy is probably done with your burgers and wondering if he is going to have to eat them all by himself."

"Noooo!" The boys yelled and started running up the driveway.

chapter

Thankfully, the first week of school started on a Monday. It was always easier to transition the boys when a normal week started on a normal day. For most kids, a short week of school, a long weekend or vacation days provided relief. But for Ricky and Ben, especially for Ben, any schedule or routine changes came at a price.

The previous Thursday and Friday Rachel and TJ had taken the boys to their new school and gone over and over what the school day would be like. They showed them their classrooms, introduced them to their teachers and went over the schedules both at home and at school.

The school staff, although willing to work with the Keyton's team that included Lori and Dr. Anderson, wanted to try things out then make changes as necessary. This was fine for Ricky who had no history of problems at school. Rachel felt strongly that the more prepared they could be for Ben, the better. With the help of Dr. Anderson and TJ's straightforward attitude, Rachel was able to get Ben's IEP updated and hopefully more suited to meet his basics and give him the added support he sometimes needed.

Rachel had over twenty years of experience working with abused kids and a great deal of her training centered on attachment issues and the effects of trauma. But as a parent, she needed the added support she found in Dr. Anderson and the insights he offered both as a colleague and as Ben's and Ricky's therapist. Together they discussed Ben's previous issues with school and the overstimulation that often ramped up his behaviors. They came up with ideas to help him cope and regulate his emotions.

Since parents have the right to determine what is in their child's IEP, Rachel insisted that Ben be in the special resource classroom as needed throughout the day. It was also part of his plan to spend the last hour of each day in the resource room to complete homework tasks and to unwind from the day before transitioning from school to home. The team set up guidelines for when Ben could go to the resource room and that he ask before he could go. They established a follow-up procedure for reintegrating him into the classroom and talked about expected behavioral issues.

Dr. Anderson was working with Ben on how to give himself a time out. At home TJ and Rachel continued helping him in areas of personal responsibility, self-regulation and appropriate emotional expression. The school, already on board with positive support, willingly agreed with the techniques recommended by the team.

The team consisted of Rachel and TJ, Lori, Dr. Anderson, Ben's teacher, the principal, the school counselor, the special education teacher and possibly an aide if Ben needed one for safety issues with other kids.

Over the summer both Ben and Ricky had been screened and tested. Dr. Anderson concluded from the psychological, psychosocial and educational battery that neither had specific learning disorders other than delays due to trauma and from inconsistent care. Both boys had attachment issues and post-traumatic stress from abuse as well as moderate adjustment disorder from being moved from place to place within the foster care system.

Dr. Anderson, Lori and Rachel explained to the staff the boys' need for the structure and safety the school environment provided. They helped develop a schedule that would be the same each day to establish security and predictability.

Lori had been right on track in her assessment of the school's child-centered approach and willingness to work with parents. Dr. Anderson offered to provide additional training for the entire school staff on understanding and helping traumatized children. The principal, John Arrow, gratefully and eagerly made room for this during one of his many in-service trainings. With the help and support of Mr. Arrow, the team set up monthly meetings and weekly check-ins for Rachel and TJ.

Prior to school starting the team developed goals for both boys and a positive behavior plan similar to what Ben had at home. Rachel and TJ did everything they could to plan ahead and set up communications with the school, particularly the boys' teachers.

With his history of fighting at school and destructiveness at home, Rachel was especially concerned about Ben's aggressiveness and violent behaviors. Rachel knew the only thing that curtailed Ben's property damage at home was lack of opportunity. There was no substitute for close supervision. The only place Ben was alone for any period of time was his room and it was practically bare. Even so, there were many times he lashed out and threw or broke things when angry or upset. At camp he fought with the other children unless closely monitored. At church Rachel and TJ had been asked to keep him with them rather than sending him to Sunday school class.

Rachel considered asking for an aide when he was on the playground or at other unsupervised times in group settings. She and Dr. Anderson discussed this several times. The whole area of relationships and Ben feeling safe enough not to fight at school was enough to question the wisdom of sending him to school at all.

Rachel brought this all up again when she, TJ and Lori met in Dr. Anderson's office a few days before school started. "Maybe we should keep him home for a year to help him become stabilized before we put him into that environment.

We could hire a teacher to come out to the farm."

"My recommendation is that you work with the school," Dr. Anderson stated firmly. "He needs the social aspect and you need the break."

"And Health and Welfare wouldn't allow you to homeschool him without a battle," Lori added.

Rachel sighed. "I know. I just hate to set him up to fail. And I hate that this adorable little boy can't be normal and just go to school like everyone else. Going to a different classroom, having an aide on the playground, all of it, he is going to be a freak. And what if he does hurt someone, another kid or a teacher? We can't expect the school to deal with that."

"Rachel, it's not all about keeping it calm for Ben. We need to allow him to grow and change and make mistakes," Dr. Anderson said.

"I know." She put her head in her hands. "I know. I just want it go smoothly and I know it's not going to. I don't want him to experience more failure. Don't you think he needs to be able to succeed?"

"You don't know that he won't," TJ said quietly. Rachel looked at him. He was fiddling with his ring and biting his lip. She recognized how seriously he was thinking about the situation and what he wanted to say.

"What do you mean?"

"At his age I was fighting at school. It didn't stop for a long time. Looking back, I realize I had plenty of traumas going on. But I didn't have a diagnosis, or an IEP. Here's the deal. I got good grades all through elementary school and high school. I played sports and I actually loved school. Even though I was aggressive and a violent, difficult kid, by all other measures, school was a good place for me to be. And I was able to succeed there."

Rachel knew for some kids, especially if things at home were unsettled, school was their place of safety. She looked at Dr. Anderson. He was deep in thought. After a moment he said, "We can't predict everything that may or may not happen. We have a school that is very willing to work with us and already uses many aspects of positive behavior support. We have a child who has some great challenges to overcome. But we also have parents and a caseworker willing to ride out this journey. We have a boy who is intelligent, charming, resourceful and full of potential. He's a survivor, let me tell you." Dr. Anderson smiled at everyone in the room. "In my line of work that is a lot of protective and proactive factors."

"And we have you," Rachel said with a smile.

"Oh yes, you have me," he laughed. "And I have been here before. You all may be in for the worse year or years of your lives but I do have great hope in this child and this family."

"Me, too," Lori agreed. "And you're right, Dr. Anderson, we have a lot of positives going for us. It's not usually this good in my work either."

So with some trepidation but high hopes, Rachel got the boys up on Monday morning following the same morning routine they had used most of the summer. Ben had been excited the night before about new school clothes, backpack and supplies but in the morning all that eagerness was replaced by edgy anxiety. When Rachel went to his room he pretended to be asleep then he pulled the covers over his head and told her he was sick. She insisted he get up so she could take his temperature. He actually gagged and made himself throw up. Ricky came in behind her. When he saw Ben throwing up, he gagged, too. Rachel swiftly herded him to the bathroom then directed him to his chore chart. Thankfully, TJ had come in from his morning run. Seeing Rachel with her hands full with

Ben he told her he would follow up on Ricky.

Back in Ben's room, Rachel tried not to look at the mess Ben had made on the floor. She hated vomit more than anything but she did her best to keep her face and body dispassionate.

"Looks like you have some extra work this morning," she told Ben. She pointed to the vomit. "If I don't have to spend extra time getting you up and dressed I'll be able to help you clean this up. But if you take too long you will have to eat in the car and I won't have time to help with this. So listen, Ben, you can get up, get washed and dressed on your own while I get my stuff done or I will stay here and we will both get you ready for school."

They had done this before. Helping him get dressed meant walking him through every little step. It was time consuming for Rachel and Ben hated it. He grumpily pushed past her. "I can't believe you would make a sick kid go to school," he muttered. "You must be the worse mom ever!"

Rachel smiled. "Probably." Let the games begin, she thought.

She waited a moment by his door while he brushed his teeth. When he saw she was still waiting he shouted, "I will do it!"

"Okay, okay." Rachel held up her arms in mock surrender. "Just making sure you don't need my help."

He glared at her. She smiled back. "When you get done breakfast will be ready. If you have all your morning chores finished in time either your dad or I will help you clean up that." Again she pointed to the vomit. Ben shrugged as if he didn't care if she helped or not but she saw relief in his eyes.

The Keyton house had pretty high standards for the kids in helping with chores. Ricky had a chore chart of simple daily tasks. Ben usually tore up any charts but he knew the list of things that had to be done in order to eat breakfast. Ricky loved earning stickers and prizes but for some reason Ben hated that approach. Nonetheless, both boys had to make their beds, get dressed, comb their hair, wash their hands and faces, brush their teeth and leave their rooms in an orderly state.

Rachel didn't want to push Ben too far, sure that his anxiety level was behind his actions, but she also didn't want to make throwing up something that worked for him to get out of school or chores. So she walked a thin line, keeping things within his control yet holding standards. She found with Ben that cutting him too much slack always backfired. He was pretty good at pushing boundaries to see if they would hold.

Rachel checked on Ricky. He already had on his backpack and was looking in the mirror at his new clothes. Rachel thought he was so cute. But all his excitement from the night before about going to "big kid school" was now replaced by raw fear. He took one look at Rachel standing near the doorway and burst into tears, begging her not to make him go.

"One more time," he sobbed, clutching her legs. Rachel bent down close to his face. "Please, Mama, one more."

"One more what, Ricky?"

"One more time I stay with you. Please! I go to school next time."

"No," she said firmly, pulling him away from her body. "You are a big boy. You will go to school this time. Look at you." Together they looked in the full length mirror. "Mrs. Brown is so excited for you to come to her room. You don't want to make her miss you."

Studying his reflection, he stopped crying. Rachel watched his face. She knew he was thinking about Mrs. Brown and making new friends.

"Okay, Mama." He smiled bravely at her through

the mirror.

He might be whiney and burst into tears at the drop of a hat, Rachel thought, but at least he was still agreeable. She reminded him to finish his morning chart.

In the kitchen, Rachel saw that TJ had already started breakfast. He was making his famous pineapple pancakes and chatting with Mary. Rachel got a cup of coffee and joined the conversation.

Mary had recently taken her driver's test. At seventeen, she had waited longer than most of her classmates who had been driving since they turned fifteen. TJ made all the girls wait until they were sixteen to start learning to drive. That meant by the time they got their licenses they were seventeen. Each had complained about it plenty. Usually there was at least one other high school driver in the house, but with her sisters all gone, Mary didn't have her usual ride to school so she begged to be able to drive herself.

"If I have to ride the bus," she argued, "I will probably die of embarrassment." She hoped to have her own car soon but borrowing TJ's jeep would suffice for the present.

"Why do you want my Jeep?" he asked.

"Because it's really cool, Daddy. I don't want to drive the suburban. You know Mom isn't going to let me take the Mustang and you have never let any of us drive the Porsche." Mary was persistent. "Your truck is alright but your Jeep is awesome."

"I don't know." He gave Rachel a wink. "What do you think, Rache? Sounds like it's all about how it looks. It should be all about safety, shouldn't it? The SUV or the school bus sound safest to me."

"Daddy!" she protested.

Rachel loved it when he played with the kids like this. TJ

had already parked her very own red hardtop Jeep Wrangler out in front of the garage. She just didn't know it yet.

"Fine, no bus," he conceded. "But I just don't understand why you want to drive one of my vehicles, especially my Jeep, when your own will work just fine."

It took a moment for Mary to comprehend what he was telling her. Her face was priceless. She jumped up and nearly strangled him with her excited hug.

"Oh, Daddy! Thanks! I was hoping maybe for my birthday, but—wow, thanks!"

"Hold on, girl, you haven't even seen it yet. It's actually pretty old and beat up. You may still wish you had mine," he laughed. But she was already out the door.

"She isn't going to just take off, is she?" Rachel asked.

TJ held up the keys and smiled.

"You know—" Rachel went over and wrapped her arms around his waist. "—you have more fun with these kinds of things than the kids do."

He hugged her back and kissed the top of her head. "Yeah, I know."

She kissed him thoroughly.

Suddenly he pulled away. "Dang! You made me burn the pancakes!"

She backed away laughing and told him she would let him work while she got ready and sent in the boys.

"I know, you're just messing with me, girl," he called after her.

"You are so much fun to mess with," she replied, walking out of the kitchen. Ricky and Ben passed her in the doorway. She stopped and gazed at her little men. "Did you get 'er all done?" she asked.

Ricky answered with a resounding, "Yes, 'ma'am." His original enthusiasm had apparently returned. He climbed into his chair and asked TJ if breakfast was ready.

Ben was still scowling. He wore a pair of his favorite older jeans rather than the new ones he had picked the night before. It was no big deal that he had changed his mind. The rule was clothes had to be clean with no holes or tears. Although he looked a little more rumpled than Ricky, Rachel figured wearing what he wanted at least gave him some measure of control. As he went past her to his seat she gave his shoulder a quick squeeze and told him she was proud of him. He paused a moment under her touch, allowing himself a brief moment of affection.

Mary came bounding back into the room jumping up and down. "It's perfect, Daddy."

"Look over by the phone. There is a sheet of paper, a contract for driving and owning that car. Go ahead and read it then we can both sign it." He had signed a contract with each of the girls when they got their vehicles. It was an agreement about keeping up their grades, observing driving and safety rules and fulfilling their responsibilities for general vehicle maintenance.

Rachel checked the boys' rooms. She put stickers on Ricky's chart and cleared Ben to eat. Both beds had been made and clothes were at least off the floor and out of sight. She made a mental note to have TJ and Ben clean up the vomit on the floor.

In spite of his bouts with destructiveness Ben was somewhat of a neat freak and liked having his things in order so his room was rarely a problem. Ricky was more carefree and his clothes and toys tended to be strewn all over the room, even sometimes down the hall. Not only did he leave his things everywhere if not reminded to put them away, he liked to have everything he owned out where he could see it. At first Rachel provided bins and storage containers for his toys and objects he collected but she quickly learned he wanted everything on display. So she traded the toy boxes and drawers for shelves. That made his room a little chaotic and crowded even when clean. Rachel had seen him go to bed with it piled high with stuff animals and other toys. They finally made an agreement that he have only five toys on the bed and all clothing and other toys put away each morning and night.

Getting dressed, Rachel prayed for the boys starting school, for Mary's first day driving to her high school and for Mary to have a good junior year. She prayed for the other girls settling into their dorm rooms, for Beth and Laney teaching and for Gracie and Danny in their big life decisions. Lord, she prayed, with so much going on, I'm sure glad you have it all under control. Please continue to guide me and pour your love in and through me. Pulling her hair into a ponytail, she grabbed her Rockies baseball cap.

TJ put away the last of dishes as Rachel reentered the kitchen. She instructed the boys to go wash their hands, sticky with syrup, and thanked TJ for making breakfast. "You ready for today?" TJ asked her.

"I used to face every day ready but that was when days were more predictable," Rachel said. "Now, who knows? In a way, we worked all summer to get ready for this. I guess I'm as ready as I'll ever be."

"I was wondering if you had time, after we take the boys in, to get a cup of coffee with me. Or do you need to get right back here for work?"

"I actually have the whole day set aside."

"Great!" TJ smiled and gave her a quick hug. Turning to Mary, he said, "Hey Mar, you better get going so you don't have to drive too fast." He jingled her new keys.

Mary nodded, threw her backpack over her shoulder, took the keys and gave her daddy another big hug. Then she gave Rachel one, too. "I love you all, and thanks so much!"

"Be safe!" Both Rachel and TJ hollered as she left the kitchen.

"Come on, guys." TJ waved his arms to the boys. "Let's go. If we hurry we can follow Mary down the road and see if she knows how to drive that Jeep."

"Wait!" Rachel ran to get her camera. "I gotta get pictures—first Mary then you guys."

Rachel ran outside, catching Mary just about to leave and had her get out of the Jeep. She took half a dozen pictures of her by the car, in the car and driving away. They had similar pictures of the other girls and there was something sad knowing Mary was the last one to have this moment.

Well, not last anymore, she thought. Her mind wandered to the boys driving and how scary their teen years might be. One day at a time, Cowgirl, she reminded herself.

The boys waited by the door. She took pictures of them together and a few of each alone. Ben never did smile in any of them even though TJ was doing his best to get him to laugh. Ricky was all smiles, but in his eyes Rachel could see it wouldn't take much for him to start crying again. As mellow as Ricky seemed in comparison to Ben, he was much more emotional, easily prone to tears or frustration. She took a couple more pictures as they walked into their new school despite embarrassed protests from Ben. She overheard TJ whisper, "It's okay, Son. This is what mothers do. The other guys have mamas too."

Thankfully, the boys knew their way around. Ben was distracted enough with all the other kids and parents that he didn't mind his family trailing along. He hung back a little at the door. He leaned against Rachel for a quick embrace. She stooped down to look into his face. No tough guy now. She saw his anxiety and his effort to put on a brave front.

"Benny," she whispered in his ear, "it's different now. You have a family and we love you. We'll see you after school."

He didn't make eye contact, but he nodded.

She watched him square his small shoulders, give TJ a fist bump and head into the room. Ms. Linder noticed him right away with a warm greeting and offered to help him put his things in his cubby. Rachel was surprised that he allowed her to help and even more surprised when he gave his teacher a charming smile. She led him to his desk near the back of the room. Ms. Linder was young and pretty. Rachel remembered Ben had an eye for beauty.

"Come on, Mama." TJ pulled her from the scene. "Ricky wants to go see Mrs. Brown. Looks like Ben'll be fine." He winked. "He wants to impress Ms. Linder, so that'll work for now."

Ricky tugged her down the hall to his classroom.

"Okay, okay. Let's go to kindergarten." She slipped her free hand, the one that wasn't being yanked, into TJ's. Once they were close to the room, Ricky ran in eagerly. His excitement about meeting more friends and his infatuation with Mrs. Brown overcame any hesitation or fear he felt earlier. Maybe being away from Ben's negative emotions helped, too.

Mrs. Brown looked as happy to see Ricky as he was to see her. Rachel could feel her tension easing. The school was built on positive support principles and care for each child. It was one of the reasons Lori had felt it would be a good fit for the Keyton boys. The teachers used logical behavior consequences when needed but the focus was on encouragement rather than punishment. This focus was evident in the way the teachers interacted with the students in spite of the frenzy. Mrs. Brown gave Ricky a huge smile, got down on his level and showed him where to put his backpack and lunch. He waved happily at Rachel and TJ as he went with Mrs. Brown to find his desk with his name on it.

TJ looked at Rachel expectantly. "Well?"

"Let's get while the gettin's good," she grinned.

They headed to a little coffee house not far from the school, one they hadn't been to before. Seemed everyone had the same idea. For a small place, it was really busy. They decided to give it a try anyway. Once inside it wasn't as full as it appeared from the outside. Most people were getting their coffee to go. The drive-through line was twice as long as the one near the counter.

It had been five years since TJ had released any albums or done a tour. Even when he was performing, he looked a lot different in street clothes and wasn't always recognized. Since retiring, he hardly looked at all like superstar Troy Keyton. His hair was shorter, thinner, and greyer. He was clean shaven, no goatee, and he often wore glasses rather than contacts. Of course, there were times people recognized him, but it was less and less an issue with the passing of time. After all the years of being a household name, TJ had learned to stay under the radar. He knew how to handle fans and avoid media attention.

That being said, people were still buying his albums. He still helped with charity fundraisers and still did occasional projects with other recording artists. There were random threads of gossip now and then about what Troy Keyton was doing. His efforts to raise awareness about mentoring the fatherless and his work with Hope Enterprises kept him in the public eye to a smaller degree. Most of the time, Rachel didn't think about it anymore. She knew he still had fans and that if he wanted it would take just a few phone calls to jump back into the industry, but her life with him rarely mingled with his former star status.

Today though, as soon as they walked in two women by the door began whispering and pointing. Here we go, Rachel thought. TJ was looking at the menu as they waited in line. One of the women came over and tapped his arm. The other hung back, watching.

"Excuse me," she drawled. "Are you Troy Keyton?"

"Sometimes," TJ smiled at her. He spoke quietly, but as usual was completely polite when she asked if she and her friend could get a picture. TJ had built his career on how he treated his fans. Rachel watched him graciously tell her he would come by their table as soon as he got his coffee. He thanked them for their kind comments about his music and he did it all with an ease and civility that prevented others from catching on to what was going on. The women went back to their seats.

Rachel thought they looked ready to burst with the thrill of meeting him. She would have been, too. TJ winked at her. Leaning closer, he whispered, "I don't think it's going to be a big deal, but if they implode we can always take it to go."

"It's been a while," Rachel commented about being approached by fans. "But I'll go wherever you go."

True to his word, they got their drinks and Rachel picked a table in the corner. TJ went to the women and signed his name on some papers they had. He posed for a couple of pictures taken with their phones. He made it look like long lost friends meeting by chance and it was done quickly. When he returned to Rachel he purposely chose a seat with his back to the women.

"I think we are fine," he said. "How's the coffee?"

Rachel nodded toward the women. "What's that like?"

"Being recognized? Having fans?" He gave a short laugh. "When you first start out you hope people will know who you are but then it gets to be a hassle. Now it's kind of humorous to me. I don't feel like I am that person anymore. But still, it is kind'a nice to know people are still listening to your work."

"Do you miss it?"

"No," he said instantly. "Well, some things." He took a sip of coffee and Rachel waited for him to continue. "I still feel restless sometimes," he admitted. "A lot about doing the music projects, being on the road and all that was an answer to what was unsettled in me. I still feel that sometimes. But either I'm getting older or I'm settling down because I am less and less excited about stirring something up all the time. I don't miss the road at all. And I don't think I could do it again, like go back into it." He seemed lost in his own thoughts for a moment. "Rache, I'm really thankful for our family and our life together but I think I will be forever indebted to country music and what it's brought for me over the years."

"Me too, Babe." She touched his hand across the table and looked into his eyes. "It brought me to you. And it's part of you and us. We have a lot to be thankful for."

"Yep." They both sipped their coffee without talking for several moments. Her mind went back to the boys and how they were doing. The kindergarten class lasted all day but only three days a week, so tomorrow and Friday she would have Ricky at home. After the intensity of the summer and being with the boys practically 24/7 she was looking forward to the school days. She needed to get caught up on her own projects, especially her paperwork and some writing that had definitely taken a back seat.

"Hey, Rache, I have some ideas about Danny and Gracie I want to talk to you about." TJ brought her back to the present.

"Maybe you can help me get my thoughts organized." He looked at her expectantly. She nodded, turning a page in her mind back to this aspect of their family that was still uncertain and largely unresolved. "Has Gracie talked to you about when they are getting married?"

"I know they are both eager to be together, to get married soon."

"Yeah, that's what I am getting from Danny, too."

Rachel saw the concern in his eyes that had been there since the day they first heard about the baby.

He continued, "I know we are agreed to stand by them, but I am just not sure how much we should jump in and help and how much they need to struggle through all this for themselves."

Rachel nodded. They had been talking around this issue. "TJ, I know you want to fix it, but maybe we need to just outline what our support, our actual physical, financial support will be and then let them decide how to best use it."

"What do you mean, like give them a budget?"

"More like a bottom line so they have all the facts and can decide for themselves what they need to do for their new family." She thought carefully about what she was saying. "What about laying out what we will be willing to do in terms of housing, helping with the baby and such?"

TJ played with the sleeve on his coffee cup. "I have been thinking about that, too. I have Danny helping me a lot down at Hope E. with the kids but I haven't fully brought either Danny or Tucker on staff. With Tucker it has been part-time because of school and now he's working at the farm, too. But with Danny, I thought about offering him a full-time position as Activities Director. I don't know why I haven't done it already. And what about Gracie? What will she do?"

"Well, it's tougher with Gracie. She and I haven't always been that close. I know she wanted to go to school. She is taking classes now but what about after the baby? Her interests have always been in the medical field, nursing and sports medicine. It's all that 'go be a doctor' stuff you filled her head with," she teased. When the media would ask him if the girls were going to follow him into music, he would always say no way. They were being prepped for medical school.

"I know. I want to fix it for her so she can still follow her dreams."

"How they follow their dreams is something they have to figure out as a family. But we can say what we are willing to do so they can plan."

Rachel and TJ considered several ways they could offer to help that still allowed Gracie and Danny to make their own decisions and start building their lives.

When they got back to the farm Danny and Gracie were actually waiting for them. Danny came over and opened the door for Rachel. After greeting one another, Danny asked if they could talk. Rachel looked to TJ. He nodded and they headed into the living room.

There had been no time to lay out any of the plans she and TJ had just discussed. It appeared that Danny and Gracie had made their own plans. Rachel, sitting next to TJ, could feel his concern as they waited to hear what the couple had to say.

"Go on, son," TJ encouraged. "You have something to say. Can't be anything more shocking than the other conversations we've had these past few weeks." He smiled, trying to lighten the mood.

"Okay." Danny glanced at Gracie. "We've made up our minds about a few things." He reached over and took Gracie's hand. "I enlisted in the Air Force Reserves. I leave the first of

November for eight and half weeks of basic training in San Antonio."

Rachel looked at Gracie, wanting to read her thoughts, but she was watching her dad's face.

"When I get back it'll be right before Christmas. Then we leave for additional training."

"We?" TJ asked.

"We want to get married before I leave so when I get back from basic we can be together. According to my recruiter, my training could be twenty weeks or longer and once we are married we get housing and medical benefits."

So many questions ran through Rachel's head but TJ was asking most of them. Danny was patiently answering with the information he had been told. They wanted to get married discreetly before Danny left for Basic Training.

"Is there a reason for the rush?" Rachel asked. "If you can't be together at Basic, why not wait until you get back, Danny?"

"It'll be just as rushed when he comes back," Gracie answered, "and with the baby and all, we thought it would be better to go into this with at least one thing settled. I want to be married when the baby comes."

Rachel was feeling the sudden reality of it all—the baby, the kids get married, Danny and possibly Gracie leaving.

"I still am unclear about why you chose this," TJ said to Danny. "I have never heard you talk about the military before. What are you thinking?"

Danny leaned forward and folded his arms across his knees. "I am not sure if you will understand this. I know you would do just about anything to help us out. We both know that. But I can't start our family like that. As a man, a husband, a father, I want to know I can take care of us."

TJ started to protest but Danny held up his hand. "Let me

finish, please. I'm not afraid of asking for your help and my plan is when I'm done I would like to still work with the kids at Hope Enterprises. But I also need to stand on my own two feet and be responsible for my family. I need to do this for us." He put his arm around Gracie.

"We've prayed about it a lot together," Gracie added. "When we found out about the Reserves, it all seemed to fit."

"What about you, Gracie? Where will you be when the baby comes in February?" Rachel had hoped to be there and was concerned about Gracie switching her healthcare right before the birth.

"We were hoping I could stay here during that time, unless his training ends up being close by. Then I could move into base housing with him. If not, I'm hoping I can stay here until after training and after the baby."

TJ had been quietly listening. He leaned forward and spoke earnestly. "I am real proud you, Danny and Gracie. I'm shocked. Really wasn't expecting this but I am proud that you are mature enough to know you what you need to do for yourself, Danny, and for your family. Rachel and I, we want to help, and we will one way or another, I am sure of that. But as a man, Danny, I respect your decision. I have always thought of you like a son, and to be honest, I couldn't be more proud." Then he held out his hand to shake Danny's.

They spent the next hour talking through plans for a quick wedding and determined that the young couple could stay in the little cottage off the patio out by the pool. TJ gave them the go ahead to get it ready if they wanted. While Danny was at Basic, Gracie could stay there and have her own space. Gracie asked if they could have a big wedding party and reception when Danny was done with all his training.

"I was thinking maybe something here, this summer,"

Gracie said. "Instead of a big wedding, would that be alright?" Rachel told her she thought it sounded good. She figured planning it might help fill the long days when Gracie would be missing Danny.

"Thank you, Mrs. Keyton, for helping us." Danny stood and gave Rachel a hug.

"You know, Danny, you are family here with us." Danny nodded. "I don't want you to call me Mrs. Keyton. I appreciate your manners but I am hoping for Mom, or Rache, but at the very least, please call me Rachel."

TJ nodded seriously. "I'd listen to her, son." TJ winked. To Rachel he said, "Took him a long while to stop calling me Mr. Keyton or Coach. I have decided to settle on Sir or Boss." Pulling Danny into a quick embrace and slapping his shoulder, TJ told him he would be honored to be called his dad.

chapter

The boys made it through their first few days of school with only a few hiccups. While they were struggling at home with various attitudes, tantrums about chores and the normal bedtime battles, Rachel was relieved that both kids were settling into their new school with far less difficulty than had been anticipated. The support team met on Thursday to discuss how the plan was working and address problematic behaviors or needed changes.

Mary stopped by the school to pick up the boys so the adults could have their meeting. Naomi was scheduled to take over at home. Transitions from one activity to the next were most difficult for Ben and Ricky but Rachel knew Naomi did a great job with the boys, especially during the challenging times. She was usually able to keep them occupied in fun, engaging activities while providing the consistent supervision they needed.

The first half of the meeting, the group talked about Ricky, assessing his adjustment and identifying areas of concern. Mrs. Brown was encouraging and enthusiastic. She explained the positive ways she saw Ricky fitting into the class and fitting into the routine.

"He hasn't displayed any behavioral issues or trouble keeping up with the other kids," she said. "Sometimes he appears to be overwhelmed with all the new directions and learning the routine, but honestly, over half the kindergarteners look the same way. He is a little immature and cries easily when he doesn't understand, but again, he isn't the only one. A lot of growth occurs in this year, especially emotionally. He does tend to hold back and watch the other kids before he joins in."

Rachel loved Mrs. Brown's attitude about teaching kindergarten. She had told Rachel when they had met over the summer that she adored teaching this grade because she had the opportunity to influence children toward a lifelong love of learning and enjoying their school experiences. It was one of her top goals, to see that her students got started in the school system with confidence, hope and positive attitudes.

Dr. Anderson commented that it would be important to make sure Ricky didn't slip through the cracks since he usually tried so hard to figure out what was expected and fit in even if he didn't understand. "Blending in, not causing any problems and flying under the radar are Ricky's best survival skills," he concluded. "When he starts to feel safe we hope he will also be able to express his feelings and find his own path."

There was a bit more discussion with the speech therapist who was pleased with Ricky's improvement over the summer. They finished reviewing his schedule and goals, then the conversation turned to Ben.

"Well, I am not sure what you are picking up at home but I think he has been outstanding here so far," Ms. Linder said. "He has been charming, cooperative and engaging—not a single incident like we expected from his history." Ms. Linder explained his schedule and his behavior plan, both of which were on his desk so he could see them all day long. "There was one near disaster about a change in the schedule on Tuesday but I think I could have given him more warning ahead of time."

Ben had argued about going to the resource room the last hour of the day. Ms. Linder had explained to him that it was not for punishment. "He told me if he did well all day he didn't have to go. He could stay in the classroom. So I had to be firm with him the first couple of days, but today he went without complaint."

Rachel was extremely thankful for the school and for these teachers being willing to work with her boys. She had hoped and prayed the first week would go well to set a positive tone for the year. She knew sooner or later there would be more difficult days.

Dr. Anderson confirmed her thoughts by reminding the team they needed to celebrate every small step of progress. He was pleased, too, with he was hearing. But he urged the group to hold steady to the plan.

"Sometimes there is a calm before the storm," he said, "and thinking there will be no storm can cause the next big storm." They all laughed. "I am encouraged by the work you all are doing. But I want you to understand that Ben's and Ricky's success this week is not by accident or by any means a measure of complete recovery. It is precisely because of everything you are doing and everything that has been set in place. So while it may look like overkill since these adorable boys seem so normal, remember it is working because of each piece of the plan. And when it gets rough—not if, when—we will keep going back to the basics of safety, trust and consistency. But having said that, I am glad we are having a good week."

Dr. Anderson would continue to see Ricky and Ben in his office on Fridays and notify the team of anything pertinent. Rachel and TJ would meet weekly with the teachers and with the entire team once a month.

As they left the school, Rachel could feel herself beginning to relax. She silently thanked God for the people around their family and the collaborative efforts being made to see them succeed. She leaned her head back against the seat, drew in a deep breath and slowly exhaled.

TJ glanced over at her and smiled. "I know. I feel it, too. It's like you don't even realize how worried you have been waiting for something to go wrong." He reached over and put his hand on her shoulder. They drove to the farm not saying much, listening to the radio. TJ sang along. Rachel soaked in the calm. It had been a while since she had heard him singing. It made her smile inside.

"You're a pretty good singer, Mr. Keyton," she teased. "Ever think about a career in music?" He rolled his eyes and turned the music up, telling her to mind her own business.

When they got to the house it was quiet. No one was in the family room or the boys' rooms. TJ went downstairs to put the mail in his office. Rachel decided to check the patio. It was still warm enough for the kids to be in the pool. When she got to the patio door she could see Mary talking on the phone not paying any attention at all to the boys. Naomi was nowhere to be seen.

Rachel rapped sharply on the glass door and pointed toward the kids near the hot tub then called for TJ to come immediately. Ricky and Ben must have dumped an entire bottle of bubble bath or shampoo into the whirling jets. Foam spewed out of the tub and onto the patio. The boys were covered in bubbles, laughing happily as they threw the expanding mass at each other. Mary, now off the phone, looked ready to cry as she stood with Rachel surveying the chaos, which was growing by the minute.

TJ came out of the house, took one look and cursed loudly. Before Rachel could say anything to him, he started bellowing. The words were mostly unintelligible but the tone was thundering.

The boys stopped playing. Rachel saw them freeze at the sound of anger and frustration in their dad's voice and the fury on his face.

His anger seemed directed at Mary. "What the hell?" He shouted. "Why did you let them do that?"

Mary started to cry and tried to talk over his accusations.

"I—I was watching them then I went in to get the phone. I only turned my back for a moment. Honest."

"I can't believe this!" He stepped close to Mary, pointing his finger in her face. "If you were watching them, this never would have happened."

Usually when TJ was distraught he gave signs of trying to regain emotional control but in this moment, there was no calming himself. Rachel could see his irritation increasing like the potion spewing from the hot tub. This was not going to turn out well. She wanted to do or say something, but felt rooted to the ground. It was like watching a train wreck you couldn't turn away from.

"Damn it, Mary!" he cursed again.

Rachel reached over to put her hand on his arm but he angrily moved away from her touch. He threw his hands up. "How am I supposed to fix this?"

He swatted away bubbles to reach the control panel and finally found the button to turn off the jets, cursing, muttering and kicking the side of the tub. Then he turned his attention back to Mary who had moved closer to Rachel. "I cannot believe you could not watch them for one stupid hour without allowing them to ruin something!" He looked around. "Where the hell is Naomi? She was supposed to be here."

Rachel was wondering that, too.

Mary stammered that Naomi hadn't gotten home yet. "I was watching them, Daddy. I'm sorry," she sobbed.

TJ hardly looked at her. If he had, Rachel was sure her tears would have melted some of his anger. Instead, he didn't make eye contact with any of them. He kept fixated on the bubbling mass still seeping onto the patio.

Finally he turned his attention to the boys, still looking outraged. Rachel saw the panic in Ricky's eyes. He was easily unsettled when people got loud and especially when someone lost their temper. He ran toward Rachel but the concrete was slick from the bubble solution. He slipped and fell, skinning his knee. Rachel went to him. As he clutched onto her, she fell, too, landing hard on her backside. Ricky didn't seem to notice. He was so intent on getting to safety and glad someone bigger was there to protect him that he was practically crawling into her skin. His little body trembled.

Throughout TJ's rant, Ben stood absolutely still except for moving once as if to shield his brother. He stood stiffly, shoulders squared, bracing himself. Like a little solider, Rachel thought. She knew TJ would never hurt any of his kids, but they didn't know that.

Rarely irate, TJ was not normally prone to yelling or lashing out. Rachel could count on one hand the number of times she had heard him raise his voice to her or any of the girls. He was firm, strict at times and swore more than she liked, but he didn't usually give in to frustration.

He barely glanced at Ricky and Rachel huddled on the concrete. He focused on Ben. "Did you do this? Was this your idea?"

When Ben didn't answer, TJ started toward him.

As he came past her, Rachel reached up and grabbed his arm. He looked down at her.

"What? Rachel, this—this is beyond ruining his damn room—"

He shook his head but didn't pull his arm away. Instead, he stared hard at Ben. After several tense moments he finally rubbed his chin and took a deep breath. Thankfully, Rachel recognized his effort to gain control of his emotions. She managed to loosen Ricky's grip enough to pull up using TJ's arm so she wouldn't slip again.

"They were just playing," she said quietly.

He shook his head again, but his eyes were softening. With effort, he tried to laugh but it came out more like a grunt. "Expensive play." He walked cautiously through the bubbles toward Ben.

Rachel could see Ben was having none of it. As soon as TJ got close enough, Ben kicked him. Being barefoot, it obviously hurt him far more than his intended target. His eyes flashed with pain, but it was fleeting. TJ saw the hurt and tried to reach out to him but Ben, misreading his intentions, fought against him. He swung his arms wildly, trying to push away from TJ while TJ tried frantically to get a hold of him. In doing so, they moved into the area where the soapy mixture was most slick. TJ lost his balance.

It seemed like slow motion. He hit the dicey area, Ben still struggling against him. Like a cartoon character whose feet were moving faster than his body, TJ flailed and tried to catch his balance. Once he realized he was going to fall, possibly on Ben, he turned sideways so as to cushion his son's fall and landed directly on his own arm. There was a sickening thud as bone hit pavement. It was horrifying.

Mary let out a loud gasp. All at once, Rachel, Mary and Ricky moved toward TJ. He groaned. Seeing an opportunity to flee, Ben wriggled free, scrambled to his feet and ran into the house. Rachel turned to watch him go and noticed Naomi for the first time. She stood by the patio door looking stricken as she surveyed the scene.

"Rache," TJ moaned, "I think I broke my arm."

Mary was crying again. "Daddy, are you okay?"

"I'm going to be fine, Mary," he said, but his face was ashen.

"Hon, can you please take Ricky and go in the house?"

Rachel said to Mary. Ricky was clinging to Rachel again. She motioned for Naomi to come over and help her sister with him. "You need to check on Ben and take Ricky to him, please. We will talk later."

TJ was trying to sit up but drew in a sharp breath of pain when he moved. He managed to get to his knees.

"Hang on. Let me help you," Rachel said. "Does it hurt a lot?"

"Yeah, it sure does. More than I remember it hurting when I was kid." As Rachel tried to help stabilize him, he walked slowly through the bubbles. Rachel prayed that neither of them would fall again.

Inside the house she led him to a nearby sofa. "Can you wait here while I make sure the boys are okay? Then I'll take you to ER."

"No, just hand me the phone. My doc has an x-ray machine and can do everything from his office. It'll be quicker."

Rachel gave him the phone and headed down the hall to see how the kids were doing.

Naomi was waiting outside Ben's room. She signaled for Rachel to hurry and pointed to Ben. He was cowered in the corner, knees drawn to his chest. Naomi had seen plenty of his tantrums, but neither one of them had ever seen him like this.

"He won't talk to me at all." Naomi's voice was full of the same concern Rachel felt. "What happened?"

"I don't have time to tell you about it now," Rachel said studying her son. "But he is obviously pretty upset." Just then Ricky came out of his room. Seeing Rachel, he ran to her. Mary was close behind him.

Rachel scooped him into a hug. "Hey, sweet boy."

"Daddy's bad," he said solemnly.

"Daddy was upset because the bubbles will ruin the hot

tub," she explained. "But right now, Daddy is hurt and needs to go see the doctor." Naomi looked alarmed.

Mary let out a whimper. "It's my fault." Water again filled her red-rimmed eyes.

"No, it's mine," Naomi said. "I was supposed to come straight home and watch the boys."

"Where were you?" Mary and Rachel asked at the same time.

"Tucker and I got into an argument and I lost track of the time. I'm sorry, Mom." Naomi looked as if she, too, might start crying. But there was too much going on for Rachel to find out if her tears were about Tucker, her dad, or her responsibility for the hot tub disaster.

Rachel looked back to Ben. She wanted to take TJ to the doctor, but there was no way she could leave Ben, not when he was so distressed. "Look, you two, we could go round and round about what should have happened here and who should have done what. But your daddy needs to go the doctor right away. I'm thinking you girls should take him so I can stay with Ben."

"And me," Ricky chimed in.

"And you," Rachel agreed. She considered sending Ricky with the girls but wasn't sure how long the doctor's office would take. Keeping the boys on schedule was important any time but never as critical as when something out of the ordinary happened. She asked Naomi to stay near Ben's door while she and Ricky checked on TJ.

Of course, being too impatient to wait for help, TJ had started making a sling for his arm from an old tee shirt. He hadn't gotten far with only one good hand. Rachel finished tying it for him then helped him maneuver his left arm into it. She prepared an ice pack and put it into the sling.

"Ow!" he said when it touched his arm. At least most of

the color had returned to his face. She noticed the ibuprofen bottle on the coffee table. Rachel scooped it up so she could put it away.

"You big baby," she teased him, kissing his cheek. "So what did you find out?"

"Doc says to come on in. No wait if we hurry."

"Naomi and Mary are going to take you."

TJ protested that he could drive himself, but she said no way to that. "Please, TJ. Stop being such a guy and let them drive you." Then leaning in close she whispered, "Ben is having some new kind of meltdown and I need time alone with him."

"Fine," he consented. He ran his hand through his hair and gave a heavy sigh. "This is all my fault. I was trying to let him know I wasn't going to hurt him, that I wasn't mad at him, but—"

"We'll have plenty of time to sort all that out later. Are you ready to go?"

TJ stood up. Seeing Ricky behind Rachel, looking worried, TJ put his hand out to him. "Hey, little man. Want to go with me to see pictures of my bones?"

"Really, Babe, he should probably stay with me and—" TJ cut her off with a look that said "I know what I'm doing." Rachel stared at him for a moment then decided to back off. TJ needed the opportunity to make things right with his kids. The way she saw it, he had some repairs to make and he knew it.

"I think Naomi will stop and get us happy meals," TJ said to induce Ricky to go. "Yeah, I think you should come with me, Ricky."

At the mention of happy meals, Ricky jumped up and down. "I want to go, Daddy!"

TJ gave her a wink and tried to shrug his shoulders but

ended up wincing. "Besides, you want to send me to the doctor with two women. I think I should at least have one man on my team." He smiled at Rachel.

She threw her hands up in mock surrender. "Whatever. How can I compete with happy meals and x-rays?"

Once everyone had left Rachel was able to concentrate on Ben. He was still balled up in the corner. When she tried to get too close to him he kicked at her and told her to go away. She could see that his toe, the one he had hit against TJ's shin, was red and swollen. That had to hurt.

"Okay, Ben," she said. "I am going to sit right over here. It's okay. You don't have to do anything. I just want to be with you."

She sat across from Ben with her back against the bed as close as she could get without risking being in his space. He glanced at her but quickly put his head down, pulling his knees in more tightly to his chest.

Rachel thought back on times she had sat in her daughters' rooms like this when they were upset. Usually she had a cup of tea in her hand and would wait it out until they were ready to talk. Sometimes it took a while to make it through the anger and get to what was really bothering them. But with each one she almost always left the room feeling things had been resolved or at least sorted out. She wasn't sure this was going to work with Ben. She wasn't expecting him to talk to her like the girls did but she sensed he needed someone close. She believed that people need people when they are most troubled. Sometimes that meant just sitting in the muck with them even though it was, well, mucky.

Ben was rocking slightly. She'd never seen him self-sooth like that and she longed to pull him into her arms and hold him. But he wasn't letting her near him. Even though he was so much more affectionate than he had been when he first came she still had to be respectful of his need for autonomy. They often play-wrestled, tickled or had other little interactions of positive touch. He gave her hugs most days without being asked. But when he was agitated he didn't want anyone near him.

She sat quietly thinking about how far he had come since being in their home. Lori told her the adoption was moving really well and would likely be finalized early next year. Even with setbacks along the way Rachel was proud of how much Ben had grown just in the last couple months. She prayed he could sense her love and warmth now.

Ben looked up, saw her gazing at him and immediately jerked his head down. "Go away," she heard him say into his arms.

She remembered what Dr. Anderson had taught her about kids saying the opposite of what they really wanted because their neediness was so frightening to them. And while she respected his personal space, she knew staying with him was exactly the right thing to do. It amazed her that he could sit so long without moving. She was sure his toe was throbbing. She decided to try and pull him out his shell a little.

"Ben—"

"Shut-up! Go away!"

Normally they didn't allow their kids to say shut-up to one another and certainly not to adults but she ignored it and keep gently talking to him.

"Hey, Ben—"

"No! Shut-up!"

He raised his head a little as if to listen to her voice. He was less pulled into himself.

"I'm worried about—"

"Shut-up!"

Again Rachel noticed his arms loosen slightly and he snuck a peak at her. She gave him a comforting smile and hoped he felt love and grace. He quickly pulled back into a ball.

She scooted a bit closer but remained out of range of his feet. "Your toe must—"

He hollered for her to stop talking but he was allowing her more words at a time. She kept talking calmly, sensing a part of him was curious about what she would say.

"I am wondering if you are scared." She was able to say a full sentence. This time he didn't tell her to stop. Instead he suddenly released a loud cry, a sort of wailing sound much like she had heard from kids at camp but never from Ben. Ben hardly ever cried out loud except during his nightmares, which were far and few between these days. His anger was his defense. He didn't usually cry unless it was part of a tantrum.

She was able to move in a little closer. If she wanted to she could have reached out and touched him but she felt that would trigger more withdrawal. So she listened to his cries and very softly sang "Jesus' Love." While she sang she prayed for wisdom and compassion. Ben continued to cry. Several times he paused to look up then resumed his wailing. The pauses became more frequent and she could see he was uncurling his body. She couldn't be sure, but it almost seemed he was stretching out toward her. She finished the song and waited a bit as he cried.

Rachel spoke softly so he had to lower the volume of his cry to hear her. She told him she loved him, that she was sorry he was sad and that she wished she could help. His crying began to wane and she knew he was listening hard to her words. He was finally calming down.

A little at a time she scooted toward him. By the time he stopped crying she was next to him. She did not touch him but was close to his side. Finally, he looked at her and didn't move away. She wasn't sure what made the change. One minute he was distraught and crying and then suddenly his tears were gone.

"Where's daddy?" he asked.

She hesitated. Would telling him TJ had gone to the doctor send him back into himself? She decided not to risk it at that moment. "Daddy's with the other kids." She chose her words carefully. "I was worried about you." He let that soak in for a moment. "Are you hungry?"

He shook his head. "Is he still mad at me?"

Rachel could feel his anxiety rising. She shook her head the same way he had.

"I don't like it when he gets mad." Ben looked like he might start crying again.

"I know. It was probably really scary." She searched his face. "What did you think was going to happen when Daddy was angry?"

"Sometimes dads get really, really mad and they say bad words to their kids. Sometimes they hurt them. Sometimes they get mad at everyone and break stuff." Rachel wondered how many men had hurt Ben in his short life.

"But not all daddys," Rachel said simply.

Ben looked at her. Disbelief clouded his eyes. Then he looked away, growing distant. He seemed to be remembering something.

Suddenly, he jumped up. "Yes!" he shouted. It startled her. Then grabbing one of his toys, thankfully a soft one, he shook it violently. He yelled at it and threw it on the bed. His eyes were wild. Rachel moved out of his way. He grabbed the toy with both hands and choked it, pushing it down into mattress over and over again. "Why are you so stupid?" he shouted through clenched teeth. "You always ruin everything!" He tried to pull it apart. When he couldn't, he threw it hard against the wall. "That's right. You stay over there, you stupid kid. Boy, you are dumber than a dog."

He looked at Rachel, his eyes filled with tears. "That's what he said! He said, 'You are so stupid!' and my mama didn't stop him. I ran to her to help me so he wouldn't choke me and that's when she threw me at the wall. She threw me at the wall," he repeated, openly crying as he glared at Rachel.

Her eyes stung. She tried to gain control of her own emotions. She longed to reach out and hold him. She could hardly stand the pain in his face as he revisited that experience. She scooted closer to where he was standing, sobbing brokenly. He clenched and unclenched his fists but he allowed her to come toward him.

Slowly, gently, she said, "Ben, if someone was hurting you, do you know what I would do?"

He shook his head.

"I would stand here—" She stood up and put him behind her. "—to protect you." Then she turned to face him again. "I would make them stop. I wouldn't let them get to you." She let her words soak in for a moment. "And if you were hurt, I would do this." She brought him into her arms, shielding him. She sank to her knees, embracing him on the floor of the room. "And Ben, I would say nice words like, 'Are you okay, sweet boy, my angel-boy?' I would tell you how wonderful you are and how much you mean to me. And I would take care of you and make sure you were safe. Because, my sweet boy, I really, really want you to know that you are safe here with me. You are safe with this family and with this Daddy."

He leaned into her embrace and Rachel felt his whole body sigh as he allowed her to hold him. While they sat, Rachel slowly rocked back and forth and her own tears fell freely down her cheeks onto his soft brown hair.

"That's what I would do," she murmured.

chapter

TJ called from the doctor's office to let Rachel know they would be home before eight. Rachel was exhausted after Ben's ordeal and she thought he looked pretty worn out as well, although he would have been the last to admit it.

While they ate dinner together, Rachel told him about how TJ had fallen on his arm when he landed on the concrete and that Mary, Naomi and Ricky had gone with him to the doctor. Ben handled the information well. Rachel was glad she had waited to tell him. As she put ketchup on his cheeseburger, he began recounting his previous injuries.

"I hurted my arm once too." He drew her attention to his plate. "Can you put ketchup here?" He liked ketchup a lot and wanted extra on the plate so he could dip his burger in it.

"Please?"

"Please." He took a bite and chewed a bit then continued his story. "But I didn't go to the doctor for a lot of days." He was thoughtful. "My mama pushed me down but I tole 'em I fell off my bike. I had this hard thing on it right here." He pointed to his whole forearm and wrist.

"A cast?" Rachel asked and he nodded.

"When Ricky got hurt she took him to the hospital and he hurt his arm up here." He pointed to his shoulder. His expression was troubled. "She tole the doctor I did it to Ricky, that I hurted him. But I saw her, she did it. She did it being mean." Ben looked at Rachel, as if to see if she believed him. She nodded. This was actually all in his file but it was the first time Ben had talked to her about it.

"But it wasn't me." He was emphatic. "Not me. I was trying to help and then she hit me and she hurt Ricky."

Rachel knew from the nurse's report that their mother had brought them to the ER and said the older boy had been playing too rough with the younger one and pulled his arm completely out of joint. It was noted that both boys had bruises on their arms from apparently being handled roughly and that Ben had the beginnings of black eye. When questioned, the mother would only say the boys were rough-housing with each other. That instigated one of many calls to child protective services and their first stay in foster care. At the time Ricky and Ben were two and three years old. The children returned home a few months later.

The incident when Ben's arm was broken happened a year later. His mother did not take him to the hospital, probably afraid of having him taken away again. Instead his pre-school teacher noticed he was holding his arm strangely and complaining about it. He insisted that he fell off his bike but at that examination numerous previous scars and bruises were found. Photographs in the file documented the accuracy of the report.

Rachel often felt sick when she read case files like his, but reading about it was nothing compared to hearing a child tell you about abuse he endured from his own parents. She had learned over the years to listen, show concern, yet calmly take in the information. While she could do that in most cases she was finding it extremely difficult to control her reactions as her own son calmly described his injuries and incidents of violence and neglect. The only thing keeping her calm was knowing how important it was that Ben put words to his experiences. Dr. Anderson did an entire workshop for therapists about the healing component of a child being able to tell about what happened to him. So while she hated what he was saying, she remained thankful that he felt safe enough to tell her.

She watched him dip his cheeseburger in the ketchup and take a huge bite. Pensively she said, "So Ben—"

He looked up at the serious tone in her voice.

"You have been here in our family for a pretty long time, right?" She figured for a child his age, especially one who had been moved from home to home every couple of months, a spring and entire summer might seem like a long time.

He nodded and took another bite of his cheeseburger.

"And there have been a few times people have been upset, right?" She recounted times when the girls had been annoyed at each other, or she or TJ had spoken harshly to one another, times when he and Ricky had fought.

Ben joined in, recounting some of his own memories. "Remember when you got mad at me for coloring all over table? And I heard when Emily yelled at Mary for taking her favorite shirt. "

Rachel nodded.

"I got mad at Ricky when he broked my fort at the pond."

"That's right. You know people get upset, even good families and even good friends. Sometimes people get frustrated. They get angry and they argue. From time to time people say things they shouldn't and many times people have to say they are sorry."

"Yeah, like Daddy when he swears. Or when I have to say sorry for being grumpy."

"Yes, everyone has problems sometimes. But in all the time you have been here, Ben, has anyone been hurt like you were by your mother?"

He shook his head.

"Has anyone been sent away because they were bad? Or been taken away because someone was hurting them?"

Again he shook his head.

"I am kind of curious about that. What makes it different here when people are upset?"

Ben looked at his food. He picked at the bun but he didn't answer right away. She waited. He breathed out slowly. "I don't know."

"Well, tell me this. How is that you can get so frustrated and mad at your little brother but you never hurt him like you were hurt?"

Ben brought his head up quickly and stared at her. His deep brown eyes were contemplative.

"He is little—he's my brother." Ben shrugged as if he hadn't thought about it before. "I have to take care of him."

Rachel agreed. "You protect him. You care for him." She smiled teasingly. "And I think you love him. So even though sometimes he drives you crazy, you are a good brother to him." Rachel paused and then added simply, "He's your family." She let the words sink in and they ate in silence for a little while.

"Am I your family?" Ben asked carefully not looking at Rachel.

"Absolutely," she said quickly.

He looked up at her. Rachel smiled broadly. "Ben, no matter how upset we get at each other or even when we don't agree and make mistakes, we are family. We take care of each other."

"Okay." He shrugged again and then asked if he could be done. She was done, too. Together they took their plates to the sink where Rachel rinsed them off and Ben put them in the dishwasher. Sensing enough had been said, Rachel didn't press the conversation any further.

She loved the way kids could have a serious interaction, say the most soul-searching things and then rapidly transition back into being a kid. She laughed as he danced around the kitchen excitedly talking about which toy he was taking into the bathtub and how great it was that he could throw the football farther than any of the other kids at recess.

When TJ came home Rachel was in Ben's room reading. She went to meet him but Ben darted under the covers. "Tell Daddy I'm asleep," he said as she left the room. Rachel just laughed and told him no way she was going to lie for him.

TJ's arm was wrapped and placed in a regular sling. Naomi came through the door struggling to carry Ricky who had fallen asleep. Taking him from Naomi, Rachel remarked on how much he had grown since spring. TJ followed her into Ricky's room.

"Is Ben asleep?" he asked.

Rachel shook her head.

"Think it will be okay if I go in and talk to him?"

"I think he is waiting for you actually," she said as she laid Ricky on his bed and slipped his shoes off. "Go on, I've got this."

TJ looked tenderly at Ricky sleeping through getting changed into his jammies. "He had a good time. Loved the bone pictures."

Rachel tucked the little boy in his bed, touched his face and whispered, "Night, Baby. I love you."

Mary was waiting by the door as Rachel came out of Ricky's room. "Mom, is Ben okay?" she whispered.

"He had a rough evening but God always uses these situations to bring about the greater good. How was the time with your daddy?"

Mary told her that on the way to the doctor's he apologized to Ricky for being so angry and yelling at everyone. "Ricky told him he was a big mean bear when he got mad." Mary chuckled. "Daddy told him he would never hurt him. Mom, what happened to the boys to make them get so scared?"

Rachel shook her head. "I can't possibly tell you everything. I'm still unsure how much Ricky even remembers but they were hurt by adults in many different ways."

"It's sad," Mary said simply.

Rachel agreed.

"On the way home Ricky was asleep and Daddy talked to Naomi about where she was and about her argument with Tucker. I just listened. Daddy gives pretty good advice about guys." She was quiet for a moment. "Sorry I didn't watch the kids better."

Rachel gave her a hug. Then Mary headed upstairs to get ready for bed. Rachel moved down the hall and peeked into Ben's bedroom.

TJ was sitting next to Ben on the bed and the two were interacting happily. From the looks of it, TJ was telling him about football. Rachel smiled watching the two of them. Ben had gotten taller over the summer and his hair, although lightened by the sun and pool chlorine, was a shade darker than Ricky's and about the same color as his dad's. TJ bent to give Ben a hug goodnight. Rachel came in the room to tuck him in.

"Mama, did you know that when I am eight I can play football?" Ben told her excitedly.

"You can play football now. And baseball," she reminded him.

"I know, but I mean on a real football team. Right, Daddy?"

TJ winked at Rachel.

"I see what you all have been doing in here, making big plans. Here I am trying to get this boy to sleep and through his first week of school and you get him all excited about football." She gave TJ a stern look.

He tried to look innocent. "No, ma'am. I was just telling Ben about our Monday night football that's starting up and then he asked me how old I was when I played. The boy is smart. He put it all together and got himself all excited. I just agreed that if I played when I was eight he probably could, too."

TJ laughed and gave Rachel his goofy half grin. Ben was also grinning from ear to ear.

"I would never stand in the way of men when it comes to football," she said. "And Ben, I can't wait to watch you play. But you'd better get snuggled back in there and go to sleep." Rachel pulled the blanket over him again and kissed the top of his head.

"Night, Mama." He closed his eyes.

Rachel fixed mugs of decaf coffee and carried them into the living room. TJ sat on the sofa loosening the wrap on his arm.

"Well, this turned out to be a hell of a day," he said when Rachel sat next to him.

"Does it hurt?"

"Not now. Doc's got me all doped with pain killers so I'm feelin' fine," he joked. "It is swollen though. I have to go back Saturday to get it casted after the swelling lessens."

Rachel asked how Ben did seeing it and TJ said after they compared some scars he seemed to be okay. He also told her about apologizing to Mary and to the boys. He felt bad that his temper had gotten the better of him knowing he had damaged areas of trust he had worked hard to gain with the kids.

"Ricky said I should have my mouth washed out with soap. And Ben told me I should pay him a dollar every time I swear." TJ chortled. "What do you think, Rache?"

"I think that unless you want your sons to talk like that you'd better watch your mouth. We could set up a swear jar, probably earn enough money to pay for our anniversary coming up," she teased.

"I know. I've been fighting my mouth my whole life. But you're right. It's not good. I was more careful when the girls were younger. Guess I've gotten kind'a lazy. Bet the boys would love the swear jar idea."

Rachel told TJ about her time with Ben and relayed all that Ben had disclosed. As she talked, tears flowed freely down her cheeks. It felt good to finally be able to release her feelings. She wanted to crawl into TJ's arms but his injury made that impossible. So she sat close to his good side and he kept his hand on her leg while she poured out all her thoughts. He offered his own sympathies. More than once tears filled his eyes as he listened to the pain and heartache Ben had gone through. When she came to the end of the story, Rachel felt relieved being able to share with him. TJ brushed away tears lingering on her cheeks.

All in all the evening had turned out better than she could have hoped. She was sure God had used a difficult situation to bring about more healing. She didn't remember ever feeling more drained.

They sat silently and sipped their coffee.

"Aren't you glad we did this?" TJ asked half jokingly.

Rachel assessed her own exhaustion, TJ's arm in the sling and the chaos of the day. She thought about the mass of bubbles spewing from the hot tub, about slipping in the slick mess and just how huge a disaster it had seemed at the time. It suddenly struck her as funny. She started to chuckle and pretty soon she was laughing almost as hard as she had been crying earlier.

It was a contagious kind of laughter and with TJ loopy from the medication, he joined in. She was glad he could see the humor in it, too. They both laughed hysterically until their sides ached.

"Yes," Rachel said gasping for breath between waves of laughter, "I am so happy we did this."

chapter

Messes are cleaned up, bones heal, hot tubs get fixed and life goes on. It seemed the more Ben was able to share about his past the more he was able to heal from the inside out. Looking back over the past six months Rachel could see gradual changes. Though there were big moments such as his experience at camp, the time with Tracker and the hot tub incident, Rachel believed the reinforcement of everyone's day in and day out love and consistency facilitated the boy's healing. He was becoming calmer, better able to focus. His tantrums were less frequent and didn't seem to carry as much turmoil of radical emotions as they once had. There was no doubt Ben was doing better, even with the bumps in the road that came sometimes unexpectedly like sudden thunderstorms. When he had first moved into their home getting through a day without a meltdown was a breakthrough. Getting through several days in a row seemed like a big step. Now they were working toward weeks at a time. But it wasn't just the lack of tantrums. Both boys were learning to trust adults, make friends, say what they needed or what was bothering them and be part of a family or a social group.

The things most children learned naturally did not come naturally for Ben or Ricky. Each step took creative work from all the adults and took the boys just a baby step forward. Rachel reflected that the reality of parenting and life kept one humble, head bowed in prayer and hand to the task. As with any children, every day brought attitudes, trials and triumphs. If things were going well for Ben, Ricky would likely have a tough day. Or if the boys seemed calm, one of the girls might be distraught about something. Rarely did a day go by when there wasn't someone in a great mood and goofing around while someone else was crying, whining or needing help.

For Rachel and TJ, this aspect of varying moods and

behaviors had been a part of their lives long before the boys came. TJ had once said he thought having six daughters had been the best preparation for one troubled kid.

The holiday season brought changes in the schedule and expectancy in the air. Early in November Danny left for Basic Training. He and Gracie had gotten married a couple of weeks before he left. They had a simple ceremony with family and close friends. Immediately after the humble exchange of vows, TJ flew the couple to the same condo in Jamaica where he and Rachel had spent their honeymoon. When Danny and Gracie returned they finished moving into the little cottage, and then Danny was gone. Gracie confided to Rachel that she didn't know if getting married just before he left made it easier or more difficult but she was trying to stay positive.

TJ and Rachel stayed on the run with doctor appointments for Gracie, counseling appointments with clients and for the boys, and Thanksgiving and Christmas planning. Rachel had worked with many parents over the years who often said that holidays, birthdays and other special occasions brought their most difficult moments.

Watching Ben and Ricky the week of Thanksgiving, Rachel worried this was going to be an especially trying time for her family as well. It was evident Ben thrived on meeting new people and the excitement of new experiences, but Ricky hated changes. He was having behavioral issues almost daily.

All the kids except Danny would be at home for Thanksgiving. As usual they would head to the Metcafes the day after for football, food and fellowship.

Thanksgiving weekend was also their wedding anniversary. Last year they had been able to sneak away before the holiday so they could be home to enjoy time with family and friends. Of course, that was before adding the boys to the mix. TJ approached Rachel about this a couple of weeks earlier. The anniversary was something he usually planned and loved surprising her. He knew with Ricky and Ben needing constant care, especially right now, Rachel might find it more a burden than a blessing to go anywhere. When TJ told her his uncertainty she was relieved. Trying to figure out how to help the kids through this holiday season meant keeping things as predictable as possible. She was thankful TJ understood.

"I know we need time away more than ever," she said, "but—"

"Yeah, that's what I thought. Don't worry, Babe. If I can't whisk you away I can still remind you how glad you are that you said yes. We'll just have to stay close by to do it." He grinned at her. "I'm working on a plan."

"No warm beaches though could make it tough," she teased and wrapped her arms around his neck. "I love you, you know."

He kissed her tenderly.

As it turned out, Rachel and TJ were right to stay home. With all the kids around and the excitement in the air about the holidays the boys bounced from one mood to another seemingly without provocation. After Thanksgiving dinner as everyone helped put up Christmas decorations the boys displayed a wide variety of emotions. Rachel hoped they could get into the family traditions and enjoy being with their sisters. And at times they were obviously having fun.

She tried to keep their basic schedule the same, but there were late evenings of watching family movies, more people in the house and less routine. It was difficult for the little guys to function without as much structure. Going with the flow did not come naturally for either of them. It wasn't all bad. They had great moments of merriment and building memories, but those were mixed with not so shining moments of behavior issues and ensuing consequences. More than a few times the family had to wait for Ben or Ricky to calm down or finish a task before they could have a planned activity or enjoy a meal. Rachel was proud of how patient the other kids were about it. That's what made the good times possible.

One of her favorite memories was when she and TJ left the house for a while to get supplies for the big dinner and have a couple of hours alone. When they came home all the kids were in the media room watching old videos of TJ's concerts and award ceremonies. She and TJ looked into the room and the girls were telling Ben and Ricky stories about life on the road or being on stage. They all laughed at their dad's dance moves on the videos. In that moment the boys looked happy and part of the family in a way that made Rachel smile from deep in her heart. TJ joined in with his own remembrances. They pulled out home videos and for another hour they all watched the girls growing up. Rachel was surprised at how long the boys remained attentive.

Somehow they made it through Thanksgiving weekend. Family and friends, eating and sharing, horseback riding and playing as well as tantrums and troubles, tears and conflict were all part of it. It was wonderful and horrible.

In the end, Rachel knew she would remember the fun times of that first Thanksgiving with the boys and she was truly thankful. But the vacation left her exhausted and almost dreading the upcoming two week Christmas school break.

chapter

The Little Girl

It came over her like a tidal wave and once she started, she couldn't stop. The other girl may not have physically hit her but her cutting remarks and sassy know-it-all attitude hurt worse than punches. She laughed when Rachel tried to slap her but the final straw was the accusation from the teacher that Rachel had started the altercation.

Suddenly Rachel couldn't push down the flood of reactions that surfaced. All the trying to be good, to suck it up, was forgotten. Rachel felt her face go hot and tears stung her eyes at the frustration of being misunderstood.

What exploded in Rachel had little to do with this other girl. It was years of suppressed emotions and misunderstandings. Once she allowed herself to be angry, to let go of the tight rein she kept on her thoughts and feelings, there was no way to bottle it up again.

"It's not fair!" she yelled at nobody and everybody. Then she tore around her fifth grade classroom like a wild banshee. She ripped posters off the walls, kicked over chairs and even threw a few desks out of her way. She screamed and yelled and cried and beat at the air. "No one ever listens!" She could no longer see the other kids or even the teacher, who must have been calling the office for help.

Rachel was completely out of control and at some level, she knew it. But she didn't care. All she wanted was to make them hear her, to have them listen and to realize she could no longer carry the blame for every bad thing that happened.

The principal and the teacher were able to escort her from the room. The rest of the tantrum was a blur but Rachel remembered thinking as she was starting to calm down, now she had done it. Probably would get sent away for this. She had never in her ten years let go of herself like that. She sat in the office waiting. Knowing her parents were coming filled her with dread. She didn't know what they would do. The fifteen minutes she sat feeling the shame of being in the principal's office and being anxious about what was coming seemed like hours. Tears occasionally fell and dropped onto her hands that she folded and refolded. The office buzzed with activity all around her but Rachel sat alone, ignored, with a heavy feeling in her chest.

Her parents entered together. Rachel could see them talking with the principal and then the teacher. Finally the whole group of adults came into the room where Rachel waited. She tried to read their faces for clues about what they might do to her and if they were mad enough to send her away. But she couldn't tell. She had only her past experiences to relay on, and from those experiences she was sure she was a goner. All pretenses aside, Rachel had shown them that inside she really was a bad kid.

She had never had a blow-up like that. Usually when things were too much to handle she would escape to her room and write in her journal. If she was out on her horse she would cry, talk, pray and vent while riding alone. And God always seemed to help her. But today everything inside came out. And she figured if they weren't sure whether she was good enough to stay, this would prove she wasn't.

Surprisingly, her parents didn't say much. They simply asked her what happened and she told them what the other girl said and how she had pushed Rachel around all day. Rachel told them about the names the girl called her and how she was always making fun of her. Rachel confessed losing control when the teacher took the other kid's side and accused Rachel of starting it. As hard as she tried to blink them back, tears keep coming as she recounted the injustice of it all.

Her parents asked if they could take Rachel home and the principal agreed. Rachel went back to the classroom, now embarrassed at her outburst, and quickly got her backpack and other belongings. Her friend Kristina lightly touched her hand on the way out and whispered she would call her later. Rachel nodded.

Once they got to their ranch, Rachel's dad said they needed to talk and she and her parents went to the family room. Again she felt dread. Her chest hurt from the anxiety of what would happen next. She stood in front of them as if on trial. She wanted to tell them she was sorry, but it was hard to get the words in her head to come out her mouth. She started and stammered and finally just looked down and said nothing.

"Rachel, come sit over here. We just want to talk about what happened today," her dad said calmly. Rachel looked up amazed that he wasn't more upset. At least he didn't sound mad. But maybe it was because he had already decided to send her away. She sat on the far end of the couch and pulled her knees up to her chest, waiting for the worst.

But the worst didn't happen. Instead they gently asked about what she was thinking and how she was feeling. It took her a while to get started talking but they waited and reassured her they wanted to hear. Finally, after many attempts, Rachel sobbed and told them she didn't want to get sent away.

"Do you think we will send you away if you get in trouble?" her dad asked in a shocked tone.

Rachel nodded.

"Rache, we don't send our kids away when they are bad. We stick together. We are a family."

Rachel looked up through her tears. "You sent John away. I got sent away from my other family and I don't even know why."

Her father looked at her incredulously. "Oh, man. I had

no idea you thought that." He looked at his wife and she indicated she didn't know either. "Rache, when we adopted you, it was forever. We didn't adopt John because he didn't seem to be adjusting. He really needed to be somewhere else. But it wasn't because he wasn't good enough. He needed more help than we could give him."

"Why didn't you tell me?" Rachel asked, feeling small and insecure. They were on fragile ground it seemed. "I thought you might send me away, too, even though I keep trying to be good."

Rachel's mom looked at her. She wasn't often tender or affectionate, but Rachel saw love in her eyes and she motioned for Rachel to move over closer to her.

"We didn't know if we should talk to you about what was happening," she explained. "You were adjusting well and we didn't want to disrupt the way things were going. We knew you had a lot of pain in your life before you came here. We figured you would talk about it when you were ready. It seemed things were going better for you than for John. When he left you seemed to do even better, so we didn't talk about it. We didn't want to upset you. We held our breath and hoped." She paused. "We didn't know you were worried all this time about being sent away."

Rachel soaked in what they were saying. It was a defining moment for her. She had never felt wanted. Maybe it was because she never allowed herself to be truly accepted and loved. She struggled with the past feelings of mothers that had turned her away, abused her and hurt her heart in deep and lasting ways. She didn't know even now if she could ever totally trust people to not do that her again. But for the first time she felt hope and the hope gave her faith to trust. It was the start of healing, giving her roots to grow and the hope gave her wings.

chapter

Christmas break would start in a week. The kids would gather again. Danny would be home and soon after their baby would be born. They found out at the last visit the baby was a girl. Gracie starting getting things ready as she eagerly waited for both Danny and the baby.

Rachel contemplated all this while she was down at the barn cleaning and grooming the horses on Thursday afternoon before picking up the boys from school. She got Tracker and brought him into the barn. Brushing his smooth reddish brown coat, she sang along with the radio playing in the tack room. He turned his head and nuzzled her arm as if asking for a carrot.

"Hey, Tracks," Rachel said pausing to scratch his head. "Want to go for a ride, buddy?" Early winter in Tennessee was one of Rachel's favorite times of the year. She itched to ride past the holler to the back of the property and soak in the changing seasons. The weather forecast predicting snow the week of Christmas. While Tennessee snow was nothing like the heavy white blanket she remembered in Colorado there was a definite chill to the air. She and TJ planned on taking everyone up to the recreation area outside Franklin to go sledding if the snow came as promised.

Cinching up the saddle, Rachel got the bridle and her riding helmet. When she was younger she never wore a helmet, but it was required for all riders at the farm, and with the kids watching her example, she wore it diligently. TJ had been the most difficult to convince. He told her his head was hard enough to withstand anything. Although she agreed jokingly, she got him a helmet with a cover made to look like a cowboy hat with a note that read, "I know you don't want to wear this. But I have to say, I love your mind and I would miss it the most if something were to happen." From then on he wore it—when he remembered. After the boys came and he could see them imitating his every move, the helmet was no longer an option. If anyone rode, they wore the helmets.

Rachel swung her leg over Tracker and gathered the reins. The swear jar was working the same way. Already the kids had collected twenty dollars from TJ. The "big, bad words" were avoided easily enough. But the boys included on their list of punishables the same words Rachel didn't like them to say. So along with TJ's usual swear words, anyone saying shut-up, stupid, "fricken" or using God's name in vain got fined. TJ always put on a big show for the boys when they caught him and made him pay up. Naomi and Mary were also quick to grab the jar and wave it at him when he forgot and let something slip.

Rachel headed past the house and hit the trail to the pond and on to the first hills. She urged Tracker to move out and for a while the only sound was his feet hitting the ground in a solid canter. It felt marvelous to breathe in the crisp air, just she and her horse. She leaned close to his neck, feeling his mane on her cheeks and encouraged him to go faster when the trail stretched into an open meadow. It was so freeing for both horse and rider to run like this. Next spring the boys would probably be experienced enough to take out on the trail without Rachel or TJ leading their horses.

Finally she brought Tracker back down to a walk and he settled into an easy pace. Rachel could hear birds rustling in the bushes and squirrels chasing each other in the trees. She let her mind wander to a conversation between Rick and Ben about girls.

They had been sitting at the table having an afterschool snack. Ricky mentioned that there was a girl in his class that he liked. Ben and Rachel listened as Ricky told them this girl was not like other girls. She liked to play kickball. She liked bugs, and horses, too. Rachel had tried to keep a straight face as Ricky described this wonder.

"When I grow up, I am gonna marry a girl like that," he stated earnestly.

Rachel agreed that girls like that were first-rate, given the fact that she and all her daughters had been that same way.

"Naomi was the best at catching bugs and lizards," Rachel explained. "But Beth loved snakes. And all the girls in our family ride horses and play sports," she reminded him. "So we think those kinds of girls are excellent. Just like your sisters."

Ben had been listening intently but his expression clearly showed he thought he had the upper hand on any advice his little brother needed. What did a mother know after all? He pulled his chair closer to Ricky's and put his arm protectively around his shoulders.

"Ricky, even if a girl likes boy stuff, you have to remember four things about women."

Rachel couldn't wait to hear this. She pretended to wipe the counter close to them so she could hear what guidance Ben would so sagely impart. She had to bite her lip to hide her grin. Ricky was all ears.

"Number one, you have to be nice to them, because no matter what, they aren't really like boys."

Ricky looked confused, but nodded anyway.

"Number two, you have to be their friend first," Ben said with a wise air about him.

Ricky seemed uncertain.

"Number three, you have to ask them out on a date."

With that statement, Ricky looked alarmed. "Uh-uh." He adamantly shook his head, but Ben nodded just as insistently.

"Yes," he reiterated. "If you like 'em you have to take them on dates and buy stuff for 'em." Ben was solid on this one and so he confidently moved on to the next.

"And number four, if you want to marry 'em, you have to ask."

Rachel tried not to giggle.

Ricky looked hard at Ben like he was deciding if this was really going to work. "Who says?" Ricky finally asked seriously.

"Daddy told me," Ben said simply.

That settled it for both boys. TJ was the expert after all. He was their dad. He had numerous girls for daughters and besides that, he was married.

At that Rachel had to turn her back so they wouldn't see her chuckling, trying hard to be quiet about it.

Riding down the narrow trail to the creek bottom and thinking about her seven-year-old giving his six-year-old brother advice, Rachel let the laughter roll.

Just then her cell phone vibrated in her pocket. Standing in the stirrups, she reached for it. The caller ID said Franklin School District.

"Dang," she said out loud. "Here we go."

She turned Tracker back toward home as she answered the call. Not surprisingly, the principal asked her to come down to the school as soon as possible. Rachel sighed and told him she would be there but it would be close to an hour.

She put Tracker away after unsaddling and grooming him. She gave him a carrot and whispered in his ear that they would try for a longer ride another day. Then she called TJ. She knew he was planning on meeting with the Hope E. staff and then later with some sponsors for the programs.

"Hey, Babe." He answered on the second ring. "What's up?"

"School issues. I was out riding so I didn't get the whole story. But can you meet me down there or are you in the middle of something?"

Rachel could hear TJ's sigh over the phone. She imagined him running his hand through his hair as he weighed his options. "Damn. I mean, shoot." She smiled thinking of the dollar the kids would have collected. "Rache, can you catch me up later? I really can't leave right now."

"It's fine. I doubt it's anything we haven't seen before."

"Yeah, but still— Can you call Lori? I'm Sorry."

Rachel and TJ usually tried whenever possible to both be present when talking with the school staff. If one couldn't be there they tried to have another person from the team fill in. It seemed to help keep everything in perspective and balanced. As it turned out, Lori was able to swing by the school. On the way Rachel called Lori and they discussed some of the behavioral issues that had increased during the past month, including quite a temper in Ricky.

"He seems to be settling in and is feeling quite comfortable expressing his dislikes. He doesn't stay upset long, unlike Ben who wallows in it at times, but he can cause a big scene for such a little person." Rachel parked the car. "Okay, I am here. I'll just wait for you."

Lori had a bit further to drive. She pulled into the parking lot a few minutes later. They exchanged hugs and squared their shoulders to face whatever disaster had ensued.

Since Ricky had never been in trouble at school, Rachel was expecting to see Ben waiting for her. She was surprised to see it was Ricky sitting despondently with tear streaks dried on his cheeks.

The office contained a space the staff called the cool-off room. It was painted light blue, was small, but contained a child-sized table and a couple of chairs. In the corner sat a comfortable cushy seat labeled the "thinking chair." The room was less for punishment and more for a child to regain control of himself. Here he could be separated from the other children, color or sit until someone was able to talk to him about returning to class. The room was visible to the staff so the child was not completely isolated. Ben had already been in the cool-off room several times, although he just as frequently went to the resource room when he needed time away from the classroom.

When Ricky saw Rachel he got up and ran to her. She put her hand on his head as he clung to her legs. "Hi, Son." She bent to one knee to return his embrace and look into his face. "Did you get into trouble?"

Ricky nodded and his eyes filled with tears. "I didn't mean to, Mama." He started sobbing. "Are you mad at me?"

"I don't even know what happened yet. Can you go back in there?" She pointed to the little room. "Maybe you can color a picture for me about your day. Let me talk to your teacher and Mr. Arrow, okay?" She stood up.

Lori asked Ricky if he would show her the room. Mr. Arrow was in the doorway of his office and motioning for Rachel to come in.

"Go on in, Rache," Lori offered. "Let me say hi to Rick for a minute. I'll be right there." Rachel thanked Lori and sat on a small couch across from the principal's desk. After exchanging greetings, Mr. Arrow went straight to the incident.

"So we have had some difficulties with Rick recently but nothing too problematic. We were going to bring it up at the team meeting this afternoon. But today it went from mild to extreme. Mrs. Brown had to have me actually come down and escort Rick to the cool-off room."

Rachel shook her head slightly and took a deep breath. "Okay." She could feel her blood pressure rising. "Is everyone okay?"

"Not quite." Mr. Arrow looked at the paper with the incident report on it. "Mrs. Brown was pushed backward as she bent to speak to Rick about his behavior. She is not hurt but he also pushed a child down and hit another with the whiteboard eraser. It says here—" He pointed to the paper. "—that Ricky threw the eraser during his rampage of the classroom. Both of the children are fine. He didn't hit anyone on purpose but Rachel, he was completely out of control."

Rachel sighed. "I'm sorry. I have seen him struggling more and more at home with this incredible temper but I didn't realize it was happening at school."

It was so discouraging sitting in the principal's office trying once again to put the pieces together about what was going on with the boys, how to help them to regulate their emotions and at the same time, keep everyone around them safe. "What happens now?"

"I would like to have Rick come in and tell you about the incident. I think it's important to hear how he processes all of it. Then maybe you can help us figure out what is going on with him and what we can do. You know, Rachel, we really want to support these kids, but we also have to keep them, the school and the other children safe."

"Not to mention your teachers." Rachel smiled slightly. "I really appreciate your support, John. I am curious to hear what Rick has to say."

Mr. Arrow left the office to get Lori and Ricky. He asked the secretary to call down to Mrs. Brown's room and have her come to the office. He sent one of the other staff members to cover her class.

Ricky and Lori came into the office. Seeing his mother on the couch, Ricky placed himself next to her. He leaned against her and started to suck his thumb. Rachel repositioned herself so he was sitting up and reminded him he was a big boy at school as she moved his thumb away from his mouth. He sat a little straighter although he looked close to tears. Mrs. Brown and Mr. Arrow came into the office and Ricky sat even taller. He looked embarrassed at the sight of his beloved teacher and started to cry again.

Mrs. Brown and Lori sat in chairs by Mr. Arrow's desk. Once everyone was situated he talked directly to Ricky. His tone was gentle, fatherly. Over the past few months, with numerous visits to this room and multiple team meetings, Rachel had come to appreciate his tenderness and concern for the kids and families in his school. He was an exceptional educator and even better principal.

"Ricky, I know this has been a hard day for you," he started. "I am sorry things are really tough right now." He waited a minute and then asked Ricky to look up. Ricky didn't meet his eyes but he did raise his head. Mr. Arrow continued. "We need your help, Rick, to understand what you are feeling and what happened. So I was wondering, would you tell me and your mama what happened in Mrs. Brown's room today?" Ricky shook his head, looking down again. Everyone was quiet. Lori looked at Rachel and shrugged.

Mrs. Brown spoke next. "Ricky, I know you might be embarrassed and I am sure you feel badly about today. I would really like to hear what you have to say. I want you to know I am not mad at you and when we get this all figured out I hope you will come back to my class and be my helper again."

Ricky raised his head a little and glanced at his teacher. "I didn't mean to push you down," he burst out. "I am sorry!"

"Son, I don't know what happened at all," Rachel said. "Can you tell us so I can know?" She had learned it was best once he started talking to keep him going. If he got quiet too long he seemed to get lost in his own emotions and thoughts.

"I—I wanted to finish my Christmas card, that's all. But I had to wait a long time for Sarah to get done with the glue for our table. So I was the last one. Daddy said girls go first, so I waited and waited. Stupid Sarah was taking a long time!"

As he remembered, Rachel could see his agitation increasing but she hoped the other adults would allow him to tell this without worrying about the manner he used to express all the turmoil he was experiencing. So far, they were listening.

Mrs. Brown was leaning forward, encouraging Ricky to keep going. "That's right. You were being very patient and a very good gentleman."

Rachel saw relief in Ricky's face that someone had noticed he was trying to be good and do the right thing. He looked at Mrs. Brown. No wonder he was in love with this teacher. At their house, Mrs. Brown had become the final authority on just about everything.

"But when I got the glue stick you said we had to clean up!" Frustration was building in his little body remembering the injustice of it all. He stood up said shouted, "It's not fair that I had to clean up when I had to wait!"

"What were the other kids doing?" Rachel asked as she gently touched his arm so he would sit again.

"I don't know. Cleaning up, I guess. But then that mean Greg came and grabbed my glue stick so I couldn't glue it. I—I waited all day for the glue and then he took it! I tried to get it back but he fell down."

"Did you push him?" Mrs. Brown asked to clarify.

Ricky shook his head, "No, I was just trying to get the glue and I made him falled down." In his mind, he hadn't pushed the boy; he was trying to secure the glue stick. Greg getting pushed was incidental. "Greg is mean," Ricky concluded.

"What happened next?" Rachel asked looking back and forth between her son and Mrs. Brown. Mrs. Brown encouraged Ricky to tell what happened. From what Rachel could understand that was when Ricky completely lost control. He and Greg both ran to Mrs. Brown and in the process of trying to tell his side of the story, Ricky had knocked her backward. That was when she said he needed to go to the cooling-off room. But Ricky, still agitated and thinking he was in big trouble, ran around the room, yelling, pushing tables and chairs, throwing whatever he could to keep people from taking him out of the classroom.

"Mr. Arrow came and he took me here," Ricky said. "I had to get control of me."

"Sounds like it," Rachel said. Just then the secretary poked her head into the office and told the principal he needed to pick up the phone. Mr. Arrow excused himself and the group waited while he listened to the other end of the line.

"Can I go back to kindergarten now?" Ricky looked to Mrs. Brown and then to his mother.

Rachel said she wasn't sure.

Ricky started crying again. "I will be good. I don't want to stop going to school!"

Mrs. Brown stepped in. "Ricky, you will come back to kindergarten, although maybe not today. But we aren't sending you away."

Mr. Arrow got off the phone and asked Rachel if she would step outside for a moment. They went into the small cooling-off room and he closed the door. Rachel felt her stomach knot as though she were the one in trouble with the principal.

"We have another problem, Rachel. Apparently one of the

younger children said something to Ben about Ricky going crazy and Ben clobbered him. Knowing you were in the office with me, Ms. Linder, who was on yard duty, has Ben in her room. The boy he punched is in the sick room with icepacks on his head and face. His parents are on the way."

"Oh, boy," Rachel muttered. "I'm sorry." She looked up at John and asked about the school policy, what he wanted to do.

"Well, I don't know how upset the parents are going to be. But school policy is that fighting is against all the rules. We work hard to teach the kids to use other resources. But according to Ms. Linder this wasn't an argument, it was a pounding. And the boy he hit was Greg, the same boy Rick pushed earlier. So I am sure the parents are going to be plenty upset."

"Of course." Rachel could understand their concerns for Greg's safety from what looked like a tag team attack. "But what do we do?"

"If kids have problems at school we try to get the conflict settled between them with the aid of the school counselor or teachers. Although Ben injured Greg, it is his first fight of the year so we should probably be thankful for that. I know we can't send him home because of his IEP, but when the conflict comes to physical contact and injury, we have to isolate him. Since it's late in the day I do think you should take both boys home."

Rachel bit her lip, thinking. She wondered what Dr. Anderson would recommend but her mind felt numb. "Okay." She was thinking about getting the boys home then coming back for their team meeting that afternoon. "How convenient that we have that meeting today. I would like the team's perspective on this. Will we need to meet with Greg's parents? Can we do that as well?"

"I'll see what I can do." Mr. Arrow promised to call her later that afternoon. "Rachel, don't be too hard on yourself.

The boys are doing much better than this incident indicates. Three steps forward, two back is still progress."

"I know but it feels like a giant leap back, especially for Ben." She realized they hadn't even talked to Ben yet nor had she told TJ anything that was going on. "Do you want me to take the boys now or do we need to talk to them some more here?"

"I think you should take them now since the teachers have to get back to their classrooms and I am going to need to talk with Greg's parents."

Rachel agreed and they went back into the office. Despite Ricky's protests that he wanted to stay at school, he went with Mrs. Brown to collect his backpack and lunch then Lori took him out to her car while Rachel went to Ms. Linder's room for Ben. Lori did more than that. She offered to take him home.

At Ben's classroom, Rachel found a troubled boy waiting with his backpack by the door. Mr. Arrow had already let him know his mother was there and that they would talk about the fight later. Ben hardly looked at Rachel when she came into the room. She exchanged a greeting and quick apology with Ms. Linder. Putting her hand on her son's shoulder, Rachel said, "Let's go, Ben." They walked out to the car.

"Sorry, Mama," Ben mumbled as he tossed his backpack and climbed into his booster seat. Rachel buckled her own seatbelt, but rather than turn the key, she turned and studied Ben for a moment.

"I know you are, Son. But I can't help but tell you I am really disappointed that you made the choice to hurt that boy." Ben kept his head down. He fiddled with the strap on his backpack and didn't say anything.

"If someone hurt you like that at school, I would be very upset. That boy, Greg, his parents are going to feel the same way." Rachel waited for Ben to defend himself but he sat quietly.

It was silent in the car. Sounds outside the SUV of children on the playground and birds chirping seemed far away. Ben finally looked up at Rachel. She met his eyes and tried to imagine what was going on his mind and heart. It was rare for him to apologize on his own. Aside from defending himself and his personal care for Ricky, Ben remained largely unaware of how anyone else might be feeling or thinking. It was uncharacteristic for him to take responsibility for his actions, let alone feel sorry about something he did. He had made huge strides in expressing himself in healthier ways, controlling his anger and finding better means of handling his problems. She really loved this boy but he did so worry her.

Ben studied her as well. Rachel wondered what he saw when he looked at her like that. It was a deeply penetrating stare.

"Is Daddy at home?" he asked at last, drawing them both back to the present. That reminded her that TJ had no idea what was going on.

His voice sounded much younger than the weariness on his face which spoke volumes about how vulnerable he was despite his tough exterior.

"Not yet," she answered. "He is working today with Tucker and the volunteers at Hope E." Rachel started the car and turned down the radio.

"Can I go see him?"

"You are kind of in a lot of trouble right now, Ben." She was perplexed at his request. "I think Daddy would agree that you need to go home. We still have to talk about what happened."

"Mama, Daddy said I could always talk to him. I want to talk to him now." Rachel wasn't sure what to do. It was true TJ had promised Ben he was always a phone call away. She said a quick prayer and immediately felt that allowing Ben to call TJ was right for this moment even though she had no idea why. She handed Ben her phone as it rang TJ's cell. Rachel prayed TJ would be able to answer. Finally he picked up.

"Hi." Ben's greeting was subdued. Rachel imagined TJ asking what was up. "I got in trouble at school today." There was pause as Ben listened. "Can I come see you?" Ben listened intently and then responded with an okay and handed the phone to Rachel. "He wants to talk to you."

"Hi," she said simply.

"So, it's pretty bad, huh?"

"Yeah. I was going to call you but—" Her voice trailed off. "Should I come home then?" TJ asked. "Or are you bringing him here?"

Rachel said she needed to get home but that Ben really wanted to talk to him. "I think it is important, TJ. Can you meet me somewhere then take him with you so I can get home to deal with the other issue I have?"

"What other issue?" TJ asked.

Rachel hesitated, knowing that Ben could hear every word. "Um, the other one." She said hoping TJ would catch on. "I am starting your way. Are you coming now?"

"Yep. Do you mean Ricky is in trouble, too?"

"You are pretty smart."

"Jeez, Rachel, when were you going to fill me in?" TJ sighed.

Rachel understood his frustration.

"I know you can't tell me right now but do you think I should know what's going on before I talk to Ben? Maybe I should come home right now."

"I think Ben wants to tell you about it himself. I will talk to you when you get home and on our way back to the school for the team meeting." She tried to keep it light.

"Okay. I am heading to the Texaco. See you in ten minutes."

Rachel hung up and told Ben they were going to meet TJ. Then she called Lori and told her what was happening. Lori had already left the house and was headed back to work. Ricky was in his room but Naomi was keeping an eye on him.

chapter

When Rachel got home she found that, without prompting, Ricky had made a card for Mrs. Brown that expressed his deep love for her and his sorrow for pushing her down. It was so dang cute Rachel made a copy of it to keep. She could not get Ricky to see that maybe he should make one for Greg as well. In Ricky's mind, Greg had been mean. Although Ricky regretted having a tantrum at school, he didn't feel any sympathy for Greg.

TJ spent an hour with Ben before taking him home. He gave both boys extra chores, most of which involved moving the wood pile around. He talked with both boys about choices and what they could have done differently. But having to head back to school for the team meeting, he told them most of the working through things would take place the next day at school for Ben and at home for Ricky.

There was little sense in prolonged punishment especially at home, which was not where the problem occurred. Rachel had found that drawing out issues only served to frustrate kids who had a difficult time holding onto why they were in trouble. Swift and logical consequences seemed to have the best impact.

After giving Naomi and Mary directives about the boys' chores, Rachel and TJ rushed back to school for the meeting. On the way Rachel filled in the gaps for TJ about Ricky's role in the day's events. Most of the team would be there and the timing couldn't have been more appropriate.

Dr. Anderson shared some insights about the ramped up behaviors often seen around holidays, birthdays or special events. He gave suggestions for relieving tension. The principal and teachers were mostly concerned with safety issues. The team explored several avenues of how to handle the next week and all the changes in the schedule due to the approaching holidays.

Together they came up with a plan to help Ricky with the transitions. They would give him warnings about ten minutes before an activity ended so he could prepare himself. If he handled the transition from one activity to the next he would get star stickers on his behavior chart. If he was able to earn enough stars each week he would get a reward at home and also receive a ticket to various holiday activities at school.

Ben was more difficult in some ways. He had actually hurt someone, which meant he had lost a great deal of trust. Granted, it was his first really big problem this year, but very significant nonetheless. Greg's parents agreed to not press charges. Their son was bruised but not seriously injured. TJ wanted to share his conversation with Ben in regard to the incident. Rachel had heard bits and pieces but not the full story.

"I know this seems like a huge step backward for Ben," he told the team. "It certainly was discouraging for my wife and me. But more importantly, it was discouraging for Ben. And that in itself is a huge step forward." TJ explained how in the past one of the most difficult aspects of Ben's behavior was his lack of remorse or personal responsibility. He always saw himself as the victim. TJ detailed Ben's frustration with himself at losing control this time and his desire to talk "man to man" about it. Rachel could feel the return of optimism to the room. TJ described how deeply affected Ben was by his own actions.

"He asked me if there was a monster inside of him. I assured him, having been in tons of fights as a boy, I understood that feeling. Although he claimed the other boy was saying bad stuff about Ricky, it was the first time I ever heard him admit he had reacted inappropriately. Have you, Rachel? Have you ever heard him say he was wrong before?"

"No, in fact he usually has excuses and a 'what are you

going to do about it' attitude to boot," Rachel confirmed.

"Ben was contrite. He talked to me about what he should have done and how it scared him when he lost control so quickly. He wanted to talk to me rather than Rachel because he didn't think girls could understand about fighting and he knew I had changed when I was kid. In the end he asked me how he could change." TJ's face grew soft with emotion. "It took me a lot longer than it is Ben. I know we have a road ahead full of turns and unseen obstacles but I am encouraged from the inside out about what is happening with the boys." He took Rachel's hand.

Mr. Arrow thanked TJ for those words and the hope he personally had in their school and the work of this particular team. "We are making history here in how this team handles difficult kids and behavior issues. I grew up like one of those kids, too," Mr. Arrow was candid, "and when I saw my path leading me to be a principal, I knew I wanted my school to be a different place for kids like me." Rachel was amazed at the support and camaraderie of this staff.

"However, we still have to figure out how to proceed," the principal said. "How do we keep the other kids safe and at the same time allow for Ben grow and change?" John was supportive but as an administrator he had responsibilities as did his staff. Rachel understood. In fact, it was his honed skills as a mediator that had calmed Greg's parents and kept them from responding with legal action.

When they were done discussing the plan for Ricky, Ms. Linder presented ideas for Ben that included being able to earn playground time and rebuild trust. The team agreed to hammer out a plan via email over the weekend. Ben was going to spend Friday in the resource room rather than in his classroom around other kids.

Heading back to the farm, TJ and Rachel discussed the family and the upcoming holidays together. Rachel said, "I know it may get pretty tense especially with Christmas coming and how hard that time is for kids with abusive backgrounds. So we will really have to work at reassuring the boys."

"Well, you know we have extra family coming in—my dad and Julie—so if I am being an a—, I mean a jerk—" He smiled at her.

She assured him that between his daughters and his sister he wouldn't get away with anything. She just reached over and put her hand on his thigh. "Can you imagine how challenging the holidays are for families with kids like Ben and Rick that have no idea why things are suddenly so difficult? At least we are prepared and we understand all the angles. Still, look how consuming, tiring and trying it is." Rachel was thoughtful for a moment. "I do my best to help families understand the emotions behind the behaviors, the reasons and the survival for family members. But TJ, no wonder so many adoptions and foster placements fail." Rachel looked out the window, gathering her thoughts. "I hope we can find better ways to help more kids have a shot at healing and permanency."

TJ was contemplative as well. "You know, I still have a lot of connections that could easily give us a platform for speaking and raising awareness like we did before." In the not-so-distant past, TJ had been honored with a Father of Year award. He had been speaking throughout Tennessee about the fatherless generation, encouraging churches and other organizations to address the issues surrounding children whose lives had been touched by violence and neglect.

"Well, I was doing more speaking and training when you first took over Hope Enterprises, remember? I traveled to all the new camps for abused women that started those first few years."

TJ assured her he remembered.

Staring out the window, Rachel became lost in thought again. It was cloudy and the air was heavy with the feel of winter. "I am sure there will be more speaking and training opportunities for both of us in the future, don't you think?" she asked. "But I can't see taking the family on the road now, can you?"

"What? With Ricky curled up in the fetal position and Ben's tantrums we could give live demonstrations," he joked. Rachel popped his leg sharply in mock rebuke.

"I'm just kidding. I know our course is set for now. Except for not being able to take you away more, I don't really want to change it." He smiled and placed his hand over Rachel's. "God will open the right doors. We both believe so strongly that kids like we were, kids like Ricky and Ben, are close to His heart. Orphans and widows, Rache. That's His heart. He always finds a way to get His message to people and to speak His heart. He always has. Hey, maybe you can write a book."

Rachel leaned back in her seat and closed her eyes as she reflected on that. There were millions of books on raising kids, parenting classes, how-to workshops. How many conferences had she attended over the years for continuing education credits and advanced training on anything from attachment issues to identifying trauma in kids? Why write yet another book?

TJ was a political science major. Maybe God would open doors on a political level for them to revolutionize the way a nation viewed orphans, abused and fatherless children.

As Rachel let her mind wander into the future, she thought about her story of being an adopted child and TJ's story of domestic violence. Ben and Ricky's stories were changing because she and TJ were giving everything in them to rewrite their lives with better outcomes.

She opened her eyes as TJ pulled into their driveway. "Maybe, Babe, maybe one day I will be able to write it. Meanwhile, back at the ranch—"

Together they walked through the garage.

"Yes, meanwhile—" TJ opened the door and Rachel stepped inside. The sounds of the family embraced her and she looked back at TJ with a grin. "From the inside out, Babe. Our home."

Epilogue

The adoptions for Benjamin James Keyton and Rick Allen Keyton were finalized on March 30. The whole family gathered at the Metcafes for a celebration, although the boys really didn't understand why they were celebrating now. To them, they came to the Keyton family on "Gottcha Day," May 12, the previous year. They planned on celebrating that day each year as they day the boys would remember they had come to live with them.

For TJ and Rachel, having the adoption completed and knowing the boys were officially Keytons was a very big deal. As the boys ran below them on the grassy hill while the adults watched from Mike and Tina's upper deck, Rachel thought about the journey of the last year and the intensity of the good and bad days.

"You know, Tina," she reflected, "It seems almost fuzzy now, hard to remember how really difficult it was those first few month. I just know, although we still have our moments, there were a lot more hard days and challenges then than there are now. Thankfully, the good memories and our love for the boys are what I keep looking back on."

"Sounds kind of like childbirth," Tina joked. "A long childbirth though." They both laughed, having experienced the pain and joy of labor.

"Yes, kind of like that."

Rachel and Tina both waved to the boys who shouted for them to watch as they started at the top of the hill and lying sideways, screaming with the thrill, rolled down. When they got to the bottom, they looked dizzy but ran back up, giggling and eager to do it again. They hollered for TJ and Rachel to come try it with them. Rachel glanced over at TJ to see if he had heard them calling for him. He turned from his conversation with Mike and motioned for the boys to show him what they were doing.

After watching their antics, TJ gave Rachel a shrug and asked, "What do you think, Rache? Should be go get dizzy with those boys?"

"Aren't we already?" she joked. "I'll go down there with you and take pictures but I don't know if I can roll down hills like a six- and seven-year-old anymore."

"I know I can't," Tina commented. "I'll take the pictures though if you want to give it a go. I'll be your moral support team."

"I may need it!"

The adults all went down to the lawn where the boys danced around their legs, begging all of them to do it.

"Come on, Babe, I'll roll right next to you and help you up if you get sick at the end," TJ offered.

"Okay." Rachel was hesitant. "Okay, boys," she said with more assurance as she lay down with TJ at one end and her sons in the middle. "Family roll time!"

"You'all are going to crash into one another!" Tina warned.

"Yep," TJ said. "We've been doing that all year. But here we go!"

Resources

The following ministries and organizations inspired some of the various programs and ideas for helping children and families in the story. To learn more about these programs or how to volunteer in a program near you contact their website listings.

Camp Esther (camp for women that have been abused) www.isaiahsranch.com

Child Help Dedicated to the treatment, prevention and research of child abuse and neglect. Organization operates a hotline for child abuse and neglect. www.childhelp.org

Crystal Peaks Youth Ranch (Ranch where children can come and ride, more ranches modeled from this special ranch located throughout the U.S.) www.crystalpeaksyouthranch.org

Equine Assisted Therapy (Eagala). www.eagala.org

Fatherless Generation is a blog and book inspired by John Sowers www.thefatherlessgeneration.org

Royal Family Kids (camps and programs for abused children ages 7 to 11 that are in foster care) www.rfkc.org

The Mentoring Project (advocates for the fatherless to encourage churches to mentor this generation of fatherless children) www.thementoringproject.org

CPSIA information can be obtained at www.ICGtesting.com
Printed in the USA
BVOW032031301011

274784BV00001B/4/P